N★C
Welc
To
NORTH CAROLINA
NATION'S MOST MILITARY FRIENDLY STATE

STOKES
ROCKINGHAM
PERSON
GRANVILLE
FORSYTH
WINSTON SALEM
GUILFORD
GREENSBORO
ALAMANCE
ORANGE
DURHAM
DAVIE
THOMASVILLE
DAVIDSON
LEXINGTON
RANDOLPH
CHATHAM
ROWAN
SALISBURY
LEE
SANFORD
HARNETT
CABARRUS
STANLY
ALBEMARLE
MONTGOMERY
MOORE
CUMBERLAND
UNION
ANSON
RICHMOND
NORTH
CAROLINA
Cape Hatteras Lighthouse
USA
34

# North Carolina
# BACK ROAD RESTAURANT Recipes

A Cookbook &
Restaurant Guide

ANITA MUSGROVE

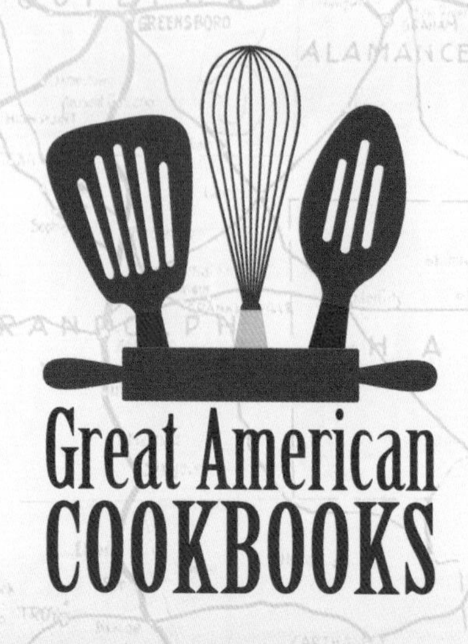


**ISBN 978-1-934817-47-6**

**by Anita Musgrove**

First Edition

10 9 8 7 6 5 4 3 2 1

Design & Layout: Nichole Stewart
Layout: Zak Simmons
Editorial Assistant: Heather Martin

**Great American Publishers**

171 Lone Pine Church Road • Lena, MS 39094
TOLL-FREE 1.888.854.5954 • www.GreatAmericanPublishers.com

# Contents



Welcome to North Carolina

# Preface

MOUNTAINS

Hello, friends. It's time for another back road restaurant road trip. Little Brown, as I call my Mercury, is just back home after a run in with a big buck on my way to work. Although Little Brown lost her driver's side door, my body man, Rodney McGee, brought her back to perfection. Are you ready for a trip across North Carolina? Fans and friends have traveled with me through Alabama, Kentucky, Louisiana, Missouri, South Carolina, Tennessee, and Texas. This eighth book in the series is guaranteed to be an awesome trip as we travel the Tar Heel State, enjoying the best foods the state has to offer in locally owned places to dine.

I have enjoyed learning about North Carolina. Did you know three presidents were born here? They are Andrew Jackson, James Polk, and Andrew Johnson. We all know that the Wright brothers made the first successful flight by man at Kill Devil Hill near Kitty Hawk. Some other things I was interested to learn: the first English child born in the New World, Virginia Dare, was born in Roanoke; Pepsi was invented and first served in Bern; and Babe Ruth hit his first home run in Fayetteville. And in the interest of food, North Carolina is the largest producer of sweet potatoes in the nation.

Speaking of food, we will start our trip this time in the Mountains Region, the far western side of North Carolina. We must stop at **Reid's Café & Catering**, where Tina Houston and her staff pride themselves on serving the freshest seafood and farm goods from local and regional purveyors. Enjoy made-to-order soups, handcrafted sandwiches, scratch-made pastries, elegant salads, house-made dressings, and so much more. Their recipe for ***Sunburst Trout with Creamed Corn & Charred Salsa*** is on page 81. Then it is on to Beech Mountain, known as eastern America's highest town at 5,506 feet above sea level, and a stop at **Beech Mountain Grille** to enjoy a yummy home-style meal, where the owners say the greatest ingredients in any dish are love, personality, and customer service. Let's sit back and relax as we eat and enjoy the mountainside view. They share their recipe for ***Lowcountry Shrimp & Grits*** on page 25.

Okay, let's leave the Mountains Region and continue our trip by visiting the Piedmont Region. **Babymoon Café**, just a few minutes from Raleigh-Durham airport, is always the best place to experience Italian culinary tradition. Their extensive menu offers a variety of pizzas, pastas, seafood, steaks, salads, and so much more. Until you can visit, try their ***Veal Saltimbocca*** recipe on page 135 and get a taste of Italy at home.

Now, let's head to Chapel Hill and go by **Crook's Corner** to sample the ***Shrimp & Grits*** that Bill Neal elevated to be the dish we know today. You will find his recipe on page 99. Crook's Corner has been described as "sacred ground for Southern foodies," offering a "sumptuous take on Southern comfort food."

No trip through North Carolina would be complete without a stop at **Snappy Lunch** in Mount Airy. First opened in 1923, Snappy Lunch has stood the test of time. Once a young man working odd jobs, Charles Dowell later became the sole owner of Snappy Lunch in 1960. In its early days, the restaurant catered to local workers and students (including TV legend Andy Griffith) who enjoyed bologna sandwiches for a nickel and hot dogs for a dime. Dowell continued in that tradition, serving simple sandwiches, hot dogs, and chips until his passing in 2012. During his time at Snappy Lunch, Dowell invented the world-famous ***Pork Chop Sandwich***, the go-to meal of locals and visitors alike. You will find that recipe on page 139; see if you can make it as good as Dowell has.

Our final leg of the trip will be through the Coastal Region, and we go straight to Nags Head, to the **Blue Moon Beach Grill** to experience a quirky, fun-filled dining experience. Though it may be small, Blue Moon Beach Grill makes up for its size with big personality. You will enjoy Southern comfort food with an added creative twist and flair at affordable prices. Try out the daily specials, cordial service, tasty food, and, of course, a "once in a blue moon" experience. They shared their recipe for ***Blue Moon Crab Cakes*** on page 215.

Ready for a delicious breakfast? Come on to Kitty Hawk, and we'll visit **Barrier Island Bagels,** where they settle for nothing less than the best. Never frozen and made with the best ingredients on the market, their handmade bagels are prepared daily to ensure the freshest, most delicious bagels on the Outer Banks. The shop also offers açaí bowls and seven house-special customizable smoothies. You'll see why Barrier Island Bagels is the best of the beach. **Capt'n Franks** is one of a disappearing breed of restaurants that once populated Atlantic beaches. What the drive-in diner was to city kids, small hot dog stands and walk-up burger joints with fresh, crispy French fries were to the beach experience. Sand-swept floors, bathing-suit-clad patrons, and maybe the owner's dog napping under an empty table were all common features of beach-front restaurants. For an experience that is second to none, visit Capt'n Franks and decide for yourself whether they serve the best hot dog in the world. Anyone that has followed my trips through our country's back roads knows I love a good hot dog.

As I finish this *North Carolina Back Road Restaurant Recipes* cookbook, it amazes me how so many diverse people, each working at diverse jobs, can bring a book together that interests such a diverse population. It does take a team to produce a best-selling cookbook series like the State Back Road Restaurant Recipes Series. First, always, is my God, who is ever awesome and blesses me so many ways, even in my drive to work along Mississippi back roads, where I get to marvel at His beautiful creation.

Leading our team are the owners of Great American Publishers—Roger and Sheila Simmons—who take a personal interest in our lives, including our spiritual life, encouraging us daily to live right and keep Jesus in our heart. From the moment the book starts to the day it goes to the printer and beyond, everyone in the company has a hand in it. It would take a whole book to say what all the people in our company mean to me, so I will keep it simple. To my production partners and office mates, Nichole, Zak, and Heather, who have a direct hand in each and every book we produce, and to Brooke, Diane, Amber, Tory, Marli, and Tasha, I give a big thank you from my heart to yours.

In my personal life, I owe a great big, heartfelt thank you to Richard Shaw, my best friend and traveling partner, who supports me through good and bad. This year, we get to enjoy his four-legged friend, Missy, who warms my heart each time she curls in my arms.

And thank you, all my readers. You are the best! This book would be nothing without you. May God keep you safe always. This isn't the end of our journey. I'm working now to bring you the best locally owned restaurants in Oklahoma. Let's eat!

Anita Musgrove

Anita Musgrove
Author

***Therefore do not be ashamed of the testimony about our Lord, nor of me his prisoner, but share in suffering for the gospel by the power of God, who saved us and called us to a holy calling, not because of our works but because of his own purpose and grace, which he gave us in Christ Jesus before the ages began.***

2 Timothy 1:8–9

# Mountains

# Hoppy Trout Brewing Company

**911 Main Street**
**Andrews, NC 28901**
**828-835-2111**
**www.hoppytroutbrewing.com**
**Find us on Facebook**

Hoppy Trout Brewing Company opened in January 2016, on New Year's Day. This brewery-pizza restaurant combo serves house-made brews and handmade pizzas that are freshly baked in a handcrafted Sicilian-style brick oven. Hoppy Trout's small-batch approach to beer production permits risk-taking not usually seen in larger breweries, experimenting with flavors from the world's hottest peppers to cake batter. Thanks to the large menu, guests can enjoy variety when they visit. In addition to soups, salads, and starters, you may also order a selection of brick-oven pizzas, from Reuben pizza to classic pepperoni and even vegetarian pizzas for the meat averse. Visit for tasty pizzas and exciting brews.

**Monday – Thursday: 4:30 pm to 9:00 pm**
**Friday & Saturday: 11:30 am to 9:00 pm**
**Sunday: Noon to 6:00 pm**

## *Beer Cheese*

**2 cups nacho cheese**
**⅓ cup salsa**
**⅓ cup beer of choice**

In a large bowl, combine all ingredients; microwave in thirty-second intervals until heated through, stirring after each. Serve with nachos or giant soft pretzels. Generally, Beer Cheese is made with a lighter beer, but you can experiment with different styles to see what flavors you like best.

**Restaurant Recipe**

## *Jalapeño Sliders*

**12 large jalapeño peppers**
**2 cups coarsely shredded mozzarella cheese**
**2 ounces bacon, cooked and crumbled**
**2 ounces ground beef, browned and drained**
**Sriracha powder to taste**
**Ranch or blue cheese dressing**

Preheat oven to 400°. Wearing disposable gloves, slice each jalapeño in half; scoop out insides with a spoon and discard. In a saucepan, bring to boil enough water to cover jalapeños. Parboil jalapeños 5 minutes; drain, rinse and arrange jalapeños on a baking sheet. In a large bowl, combine cheese, bacon and beef; mix in sriracha powder. Generously sprinkle cheese mixture into jalapeño halves. Bake 5 to 7 minutes or until cheese is lightly browned on top. Serve with ranch or blue cheese dressing.

**Restaurant Recipe**

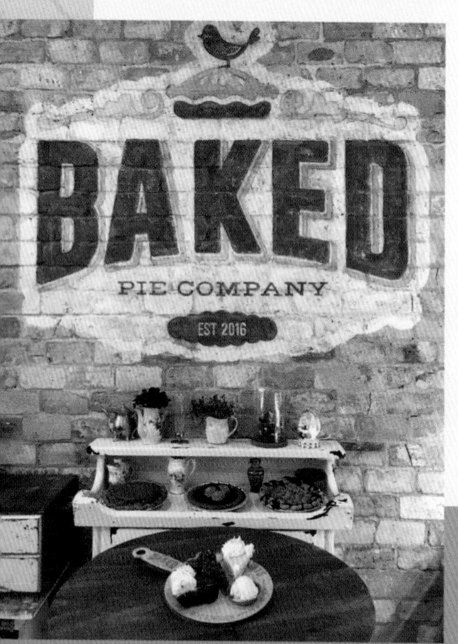

**4 Long Shoals Road**
**Arden, NC 28704**
**828-333-4366**

**50 North Merrimon Avenue, Suite 103**
**Asheville, NC 28804**
**828-210-9544**
**www.bakedpiecompany.com • Find us on Facebook**

In the summer of 2016, Kirsten and her daughter were looking for a place in south Asheville to enjoy a slice of homemade blueberry pie and a cup of coffee. Search as they might, they found no such place. Inspired by her background in business management and a love of all things baked, Kirsten began to search for a location, a baker, and a network of local suppliers to turn her idea into a reality. Today, Baked Pie Company is a place where everyone is welcome to dig into one of the bakery's scrumptious pies. At Baked Pie Company, the staff strive to make you smile and feel at home.

**Tuesday – Thursday: 10:00 am to 8:00 pm**
**Friday & Saturday: 10:00 am to 9:00 pm**
**Sunday: 11:00 am to 4:00 pm**

## *Tart Lemon Chess Pie*

**½ cup melted butter**
**1½ cups sugar**
**2 teaspoons lemon zest**
**1½ tablespoons cornstarch**
**¼ teaspoon sea salt**
**1 tablespoon cornmeal**
**¾ cup lemon juice**
**4 eggs**
**1 (9-inch) pie crust**
**Powdered sugar for dusting**

Preheat oven to 350°. In a bowl, whisk together all ingredients except eggs. Add eggs one at a time, mixing after each addition until incorporated. Pour filling into unbaked pie shell. Bake 45 minutes until set. Cool completely, then dust generously with powdered sugar before serving.

**Restaurant Recipe**

## *Aunt Margaret's Peach Cobbler*

**2 cups peeled and sliced peaches**
**1 cup plus 2 tablespoons sugar, divided**
**1 cup plus 1 tablespoon flour, divided**
**1 stick butter**
**1 cup milk**
**½ teaspoon sea salt**
**2 teaspoons baking powder**

Preheat oven to 350°. In a bowl, mix together peaches, 2 tablespoons sugar and 1 tablespoon flour; set aside 30 minutes. Add butter to a 7x11-inch baking dish and place in oven to melt. In another bowl, mix remaining ingredients; remove dish from oven and add flour mixture over top of melted butter. Pour peaches over top of flour mixture. Return to oven, baking 40 to 50 minutes or until browned on top. Serve warm.

**Family Favorite**

# Ivory Road Café & Kitchen

**1854 Brevard Road**
**Arden, NC 28704**
**828-676-3870**
**www.ivoryroadavl.com • Find us on Facebook**

Opened in August 2016, Ivory Road Café & Kitchen is the culmination of a lifelong love of food and culture. This local, independent restaurant, bakery, and tea room serves up all-day breakfast, quiche, homemade soups and baked goods, and more. Owner Jill named the restaurant after the street she grew up on. Since leaving the "real" Ivory Road, Jill has traveled the world in pursuit of the exotic, the simple, and everything in between. She credits her time spent working as a pastry cook in an upscale, fine-dining restaurant in Melbourne, Australia, for waking her to the reality that "food is a lifelong learning journey."

**Monday & Tuesday:**
**9:00 am to 4:00 pm**
**Wednesday, Thursday & Friday:**
**9:00 am to 9:00 pm**
**Saturday: 9:00 am to 1:00 pm**
**Afternoon Tea:**
**Saturday: 2:00 pm**

## *Pimento Cheese*

**1 (8-ounce) package cream cheese, softened**
**1 cup mayonnaise**
**2 tablespoons whole-grain mustard**
**2 tablespoons adobo sauce**
**1 tablespoon chopped dill**
**8 ounces pimento peppers, roughly chopped**
**2 pounds grated cheese blend (sharp Cheddar, Monterey Jack and Swiss)**

In a bowl, use an electric mixer to combine cream cheese, mayonnaise, mustard, adobo and dill. Add pimentos and cheese; fold together with hands or a spatula. Serve with crackers and sliced veggies or on a panini.

Restaurant Recipe

## *Corn Puddin' Crab Cakes*

**8 ounces jumbo lump crabmeat**
**¼ cup sweet whole-kernel corn**
**1 teaspoon whole-grain mustard**
**½ teaspoon lemon juice**
**1 teaspoon Worcestershire sauce**
**2 teaspoons Old Bay seasoning**
**2 tablespoons browned butter**
**1 tablespoon mayonnaise**
**1 tablespoon cornmeal, plus extra for coating**
**2 eggs**

Combine all ingredients in a bowl, mixing thoroughly with hands or spatula. Form cakes of desired size with hands or a scoop, packing tightly to ensure they maintain their shape. Coat cakes with extra cornmeal. Sear in a hot skillet over medium-high heat until golden brown on each side, flipping once. Place on a cookie sheet and finish baking at 325° until a thermometer inserted in center of cakes reads 160°. Enjoy with a squeeze of lemon juice or remoulade sauce.

Restaurant Recipe

# Eat Crow

**9872 Highway 105 South**
**Banner Elk, NC 28604**
**828-963-8228**
**www.eatcrownc.com • Find us on Facebook**

Eat Crow is a quaint café and bakery owned and operated by Dominic and Meryle Geraghty and their dedicated staff. Dom has been an executive chef for more than thirty years, serving delicacies in places like New Mexico, Alaska, California, Massachusetts, Scotland, and his native home of England. In 2011, he opened Eat Crow after working for years at several other North Carolina eateries. Meryle played a vital part as well in the opening of Eat Crow, providing eclectic vision and inspiration without which the restaurant would never have existed. Stop by today for a gourmet lunch, delectable sweet treats, or custom catering. Eat Pie; Eat Cake; Eat Crow!

**Tuesday – Saturday: 10:00 am to 4:00 pm**
**Lunch:**
**11:00 am to 3:00 pm**

**Call for Dinner Schedule and Reservations**

# Pear & Chocolate Tart

### *Sweet Pastry Crust:*

**¾ cup sugar**
**3½ unsalted butter, softened**
**1 egg**
**1 teaspoon vanilla extract**
**1 pound pastry flour**

In a stand mixer with a dough hook attachment, add sugar, butter, egg and vanilla; mix at low speed just until blended. Add flour and continue mixing until smooth. Cover bowl with plastic wrap and refrigerate dough 30 minutes. Roll out dough to fit a 10-inch springform as well as come halfway up sides. Spray pan with nonstick spray and line with dough, making sure there are no cracks or tears.

### *Filling:*

**2 ripe Bosc or Bartlett pears with stems on**
**1 egg plus 3 egg yolks, divided**
**1 cup sugar**
**1½ cups heavy cream**
**1 teaspoon vanilla extract**
**4 ounces semisweet chocolate chips**
**½ cup or less orange marmalade, heated**

Preheat oven to 350°. Remove top of one of pears for garnish, cutting about 1½ inches down; set aside. Core rest of pear and remaining pear, then neatly slice. In a bowl, mix eggs, sugar, cream and vanilla until well blended. Evenly sprinkle chocolate chips over tart crust; layer sliced pears next. Pour custard over top of pears, then place garnishing pear top in center of tart. Bake about 50 minutes or until custard is set. Refrigerate 1 hour or until completely cold. To serve, heat in oven 2 minutes to loosen springform pan, unclip and gently remove. Serve on a cake board or flat plate and drizzle with marmalade.

**Restaurant Recipe**

# The Painted Fish Café & Beer Bar

**2941 Tynecastle Highway**
**Banner Elk, NC 28604**
**828-898-6800**
**www.paintedfishcafe.com • Find us on Facebook**

Step inside The Painted Fish Café & Beer Bar and discover something truly unique: recognizable dishes with a twist. Enjoy an upscale experience in relaxed, casual ambience while you indulge in tasty dishes like jalapeño crab cakes and Southern-style chicken carbonara. Good food is nothing without something spectacular to wash it down. The Beer Bar offers a continually evolving array of artisanal beers, from lagers to stouts. You can also sample a selection of boutique wines or fine spirits. Heated outdoor dining includes a beautiful view at the foot of Sugar Mountain Ski Resort. Visit The Painted Fish Café & Beer Bar for inspired food for family and friends.

Dinner:
**Monday – Saturday: 5:00 pm to 9:00 pm**
Lunch:
**Friday & Saturday: 11:00 am to 2:00 pm**
Brunch:
**Sunday: 11:00 am to 2:00 pm**

## *Barbecued Country-Style Pork Ribs*

**5 pounds country-style pork ribs**
**6 tablespoons butter, divided**
**½ cup chopped onions**
**1 tablespoon paprika**
**½ teaspoon black pepper**
**¼ cup sugar**
**1 teaspoon mustard**
**2 teaspoons Tabasco sauce**
**¼ cup ketchup**
**5 tablespoons apple cider vinegar**

Preheat oven to 350°. Place ribs in large baking pan; dot with 3 tablespoons butter. Place in oven; make sauce. In a saucepan over medium heat, melt remaining butter; add onions, cooking until translucent. Add remaining ingredients; simmer 20 minutes. Periodically baste ribs with sauce, cooking 1 hour or until tender.

**Local Favorite**

## *Mud Hens*

**1½ cups all-purpose flour**
**1 teaspoon baking powder**
**Pinch salt**
**1 cup sugar**
**1 stick butter, softened**
**3 eggs, separated**
**1 teaspoon vanilla**
**1 pound brown sugar**
**1 teaspoon lemon juice**
**1 cup crushed nuts**
**Whipped cream for topping**

Preheat oven to 375°. In a bowl, sift together flour, baking powder and salt; set aside. Using an electric mixer, cream together sugar and butter in a bowl. Add 3 egg yolks and 1 egg white; mix well. Add flour mixture and vanilla; mix. Grease and flour an 11.5x17.5-inch cookie sheet; evenly pat dough into pan. In another bowl, whisk together brown sugar, lemon juice and 2 egg whites; spread evenly over dough. Sprinkle with nuts. Bake 20 minutes. Cut into 35 squares. Serve topped with whipped cream.

**Local Favorite**

# Stonewalls Restaurant

**344 Shawneehaw Avenue South**
**Banner Elk, NC 28604**
**828-898-5550**
**www.stonewallsrestaurant.com • Find us on Facebook**

Stonewalls Restaurant serves prime rib, seafood, and gourmet steaks as well as fine wines, olive oils, and balsamics. Located in Downtown Banner Elk, Stonewalls Restaurant has been locally owned and operated since 1985. The restaurant prides itself on exceptional service and value. Dine on the finest cuts of beef found in prime rib, sirloin, rib eye, New York strip, and filet mignon. The chicken and ribs are second to none, and the restaurant also has a great lineup of seafood. The salad bar is a destination for locals and tourists. Stonewalls Restaurant's staff look forward to hosting you soon.

**Dinner:**
**Daily: 5:00 pm to 9:00 pm**
**Brunch:**
**Sunday: 10:00 am to 2:00 pm**

## Red Velvet Cheesecake Cake

### Red Velvet Layers:

**2½ cups all-purpose flour**
**1½ cups sugar**
**1 teaspoon baking soda**
**1 teaspoon salt**
**¼ cup unsweetened cocoa powder**
**¾ cup vegetable oil**
**1 cup buttermilk**
**2 large eggs**
**2 tablespoons red food coloring**
**1 teaspoon white vinegar**
**1 teaspoon vanilla extract**

Preheat oven to 350°. Grease and flour two 8-inch square pans. Sift together dry ingredients. Whisk in remaining ingredients until smooth. Divide batter between pans; bake 30 to 35 minutes. Cool to room temperature, invert onto a parchment-lined cookie sheet and refrigerate.

### Cheesecake Layer:

**2 (8-ounce) packages cream cheese, softened**
**7 ounces sweetened condensed milk**
**2 tablespoons flour**
**2 large eggs**
**1 teaspoon vanilla extract**

Grease and flour one 8-inch square pan. In an electric mixer, beat cream cheese until smooth. Beat in flour and condensed milk. Beat in eggs, one at a time. Stir in vanilla. Transfer mixture to pan; bake at 350° for 10 to 15 minutes. Cool to room temperature, invert onto a parchment-lined cookie sheet and refrigerate.

### Cream Cheese Frosting:

**2 (8-ounce) packages cream cheese, softened**
**½ cup butter, softened**
**1¾ pounds powdered sugar**
**1 teaspoon vanilla extract**

In an electric mixer, beat cream cheese and butter; beat in powdered sugar a little at a time until smooth. Beat in vanilla. To assemble: place a red velvet layer on a cake plate. Frost with ½ cup frosting. Place cheesecake layer on top of first layer; frost with ½ cup frosting. Top with remaining red velvet layer; frost outside of cake with remaining frosting. Refrigerate before serving.

Restaurant Recipe

## Wild Mushroom Pasta

**3 tablespoons mushroom sage olive oil**
**2 cups sliced mushrooms**
**½ cup heavy cream**
**¾ teaspoon truffle salt**
**16 ounces cooked pasta**

In a skillet over medium heat, add oil; add mushrooms and sauté until tender. Add cream; bring to a boil. Reduce slightly, then add truffle salt and pasta. Cook until heated through. Serves 2 to 4.

Restaurant Recipe

**502 Beech Mountain Parkway**
**Beech Mountain, NC 28604**
**828-387-4900**
**www.beechmountaingrille.com**
**Find us on Facebook**

When it comes to restaurant and bar services, Beech Mountain Grille is expressively creative and deliberately original. The chef and culinary staff know exactly what it takes to create outstanding menus and provide impeccable service that compliments every dish and drink. Specializing in casual comfort food, including lunch and dinner as well as catering, parties, and casual dining, Beech Mountain Grille can make your next meal one you and your family won't forget. Drop by for home-style meals, a full-service bar, the comfy atmosphere, and a fantastic mountainside view. At Beech Mountain Grille, the greatest ingredients are love, personality, and customer service.

**Seasonal Hours Vary Each Month**

## *Lowcountry Shrimp & Grits*

**½ cup stone-ground grits**
**Salt to taste**
**2 tablespoons butter**
**Olive oil to taste**
**Blackening seasoning to taste**
**2 cups heavy cream**
**2 tablespoons Cajun seasoning**
**Powdered Parmesan cheese to taste**
**6 jumbo shrimp, peeled and deveined**
**House-Made Bruschetta**

In a saucepan, bring 2 cups water to a boil; add salt and grits and cook, stirring frequently, about 8 to 10 minutes. Stir in butter; set aside. Preheat grill to 400°; drizzle shrimp with oil, skewer, sprinkle with blackening seasoning and grill 2 to 3 minutes each side or until pink. In a saucepan, stir together cream and Cajun seasoning; bring to a boil, then reduce heat. Stir in Parmesan and shrimp. Ladle grits into a bowl, add shrimp and sauce and top with House-Made Bruschetta.

**Restaurant Recipe**

## *House-Made Bruschetta*

**4 large big beef tomatoes**
**1 small onion**
**2 tablespoons chopped garlic**
**2 tablespoons chopped fresh basil**
**2 tablespoons olive oil**
**Feta cheese to taste**
**Balsamic vinegar**
**Balsamic glaze**

Chop tomatoes and onion; toss with garlic, basil and oil in a bowl. Top with feta. In another bowl, mix 3 parts balsamic vinegar to 1 part balsamic glaze; drizzle over Bruschetta. Serve over Lowcountry Shrimp & Grits.

**Restaurant Recipe**

# Holy Smokes BBQ

**3363 Beech Mountain Parkway**
**Beech Mountain, NC 28604**
**828-387-4200**
**www.whitewolfbeechmountain.com • Find us on Facebook**

Holy Smokes BBQ at White Wolf Lodge on Beech Mountain serves up delicious barbecue that will keep you coming back again and again. This mountainside eatery knows how to do barbecue just right. Stop in to sample the apple butter barbecue sauce on a perfectly smoked pulled pork sandwich. You might also try the half-pound plate of smoke sausage. If you've arrived at Beech Mountain for a walk on the wild side, don't forget to order the BBQ Wolfdog, which is a standard hot dog topped with pulled pork and cheese. You can't go wrong. Drop by Holy Smokes BBQ at White Wolf Lodge today. You won't be disappointed.

**Thursday – Saturday: 11:00 am to 8:00 pm**

## *Potato Soup*

**5 pounds potatoes, peeled and diced**
**2 onions, diced**
**1 stick butter**
**1 tablespoon salt**
**1 tablespoon seasoning salt**
**1 teaspoon garlic powder**
**1 teaspoon white pepper**
**¾ cup flour**
**1 quart heavy cream**

Add potatoes and onions to a stockpot; cover with water. Add butter, salt, seasoning salt, garlic powder and white pepper. Bring to a boil and cook 15 minutes or until potatoes are fork tender. In a bowl, make a paste with flour and cream; stir into pot and cook until thickened.

**Restaurant Recipe**

# Foggy Rock Eatery & Pub

**8180 Valley Boulevard**
**Blowing Rock, NC 28605**
**828-295-7262**
**www.foggy-rock.com • Find us on Facebook**

Foggy Rock Eatery & Pub is a local, family-owned restaurant established in late 2010. The restaurant strives to be a part of the community, serving both locals and visitors in its beautiful mountain village. With a passion for food, Foggy Rock offers a "twist on the ordinary," serving everyday classics in its own unique style. Constantly looking for new trends, the restaurant doesn't limit the menu to a specific cuisine. At Foggy Rock, it's believed that all the different cooking styles of the world are equally tasty. Foggy Rock Eatery & Pub relies on word of mouth. If your enjoyed your experience, please be sure to spread the word!

**Daily: 11:30 am to 9:00 pm**

## *Avocado Eggrolls*

**15 ripe avocados, pits and skins removed**
**1 red onion, diced**
**8 cups black bean and corn salsa**
**4 cups shredded Jack cheese**
**4 cups shredded Cheddar cheese**
**4 cups whipped cream cheese**
**2 cups Roland's sweet chili sauce**
**Panko breadcrumbs to taste**
**Eggroll wrappers**

Rough chop avocado, then mix with remaining ingredients except wrappers in a large bowl, smashing avocados as you mix. To assemble: lay out eggroll wrapper with a corner pointed toward you. Place ¼ cup avocado mixture onto wrapper; sprinkle flour on board, then fold in left and right corners and roll up. Seal edges with water. Fry in deep fryer until golden brown.

**Restaurant Recipe**

## *Pimento Cheese*

**8 cups shredded Cheddar cheese**
**4 cups shredded mozzarella cheese**
**1 cup Texas Pete wing sauce**
**3 cups heavy mayonnaise**
**2 cups diced roasted red peppers with juice**
**1 cup cream cheese**

In a large bowl, combine cheeses, mayonnaise and Texas Pete. Blend red peppers and juice in a food processor with cream cheese until combined; transfer to bowl with cheese mixture and mix with hands. Serve with warm pita, on sliders with bacon, on a burger, or so much more.

**Restaurant Recipe**

# Casa Rustica

**1348 Highway 105 South**
**Boone, NC 28607**
**828-262-5128**
**www.casarustica1981.com**
**Find us on Facebook**

Opened by Peter and Sara Pedroni in 1981, Casa Rustica fuses Old-World Italian cuisine with the fresh flavors of North Carolina. In 2004, Peter and Sara retired, passing their culinary legacy to their son, Ricky, and his wife, Liz. Since opening, Casa Rustica has become one of the most beloved restaurants in the area, featuring global Italian fare with intimate fireside dining. The restaurant also offers a unique space and custom-catered menus for private events and features live music in season, from jazz to classical guitar. Casa Rustica is the perfect place to enjoy friends, family, and the bold flavors of Italy. "Buon Cibo, Buon Vino, Buoni Amici!"

**Monday – Thursday: 5:00 pm to 9:30 pm**
**Friday & Saturday: 5:00 pm 10:00 pm**
**Sunday: 5:00 pm to 9:00 pm**

## *Steak Pina*

*This recipe is named after Rick's grandmother in Italy. It's simple but great!*

**1 hand-cut, aged, certified Angus steak of choice (filet, ribeye or New York strip)**
**2 to 3 tablespoons light olive oil**
**Salt and pepper to taste**

Roll steak in light olive oil, then season to taste with salt and pepper. Grill to desired doneness or slightly under. Rest while preparing Pina Sauce.

### *Pina Sauce:*

**1½ teaspoons butter**
**Chopped garlic, dry chives and light red pepper to taste**
**1½ teaspoons oil**
**Button mushrooms, sliced**
**2 tablespoons brandy**
**½ cup heavy cream**
**Salt and pepper to taste**
**1 tablespoon red pepper vinegar sauce**

Whip together butter, garlic, chives and red pepper; add to skillet with oil. Add mushrooms, then sauté 1½ minutes, taking care not to overcook or brown butter. Remove from heat and stir in brandy; quickly return to heat (be prepared for light flames if cooking with gas) and reduce 1 to 2 minutes. Slowly drizzle in heavy cream, shifting and folding with a spatula as you pour. Allow to thicken; season with salt, pepper and red pepper vinegar. Coat steak and serve with a glass of chianti or dry red Italian wine.

**Restaurant Recipe**

# F.A.R.M. CAFE

*Feed All Regardless of Means*

## REAL. GOOD. FOOD.

**617 West King Street**
**Boone, NC 28607**
**828-386-1000**
**www.farmcafe.org • Find us on Facebook**

Opened in May 2012, F.A.R.M. Café is a nonprofit, pay-what-you-can community kitchen that operates in accordance with one mantra: "Feed All Regardless of Means." In pursuit of building a healthy and inclusive community, it is the stated vision of F.A.R.M. Café to eliminate hunger in the surrounding community. The café provides high-quality, delicious meals made from locally sourced ingredients. F.A.R.M. Café serves people from all walks of life, from patrons in need to pay-it-forward patrons who selflessly pay more than the suggested donation to cover the cost of those who cannot pay at all. Eat at F.A.R.M Café for real good food with a real good community in mind.

**Monday – Friday: 11:00 am to 2:00 pm**

## Carrot-Ginger Soup

*This light, coconut-infused carrot soup is a café favorite with the addition of ginger and Chinese five spice.*

**1 cup minced onion**
**2 tablespoons minced garlic**
**2 tablespoons canola oil**
**2 quarts vegetable stock**
**6 cups peeled, diced carrots**
**1 teaspoon Chinese five spice powder**
**4 cups coconut milk**
**4 makrut leaves or 2 limes, zested and juiced**
**¼ cup minced fresh ginger**
**1 lemon, juiced**
**Kosher salt and white pepper to taste**

In a saucepan over medium heat, sauté onion and garlic in oil until translucent. Add stock and carrots; bring to a boil. Reduce heat to medium-low, add Chinese five spice and simmer 30 minutes until carrots are tender. In a small stockpot over low heat, add coconut milk, makrut leaves and ginger; bring to a simmer, remove from heat and cover to steep 30 to 45 minutes. Strain milk through a sieve; set aside. Purée soup with an immersion blender, slowly adding coconut milk. Once blended, season with salt and pepper.

**Restaurant Recipe**

## Tomato Pie

**3 to 4 large heirloom tomatoes**
**1 teaspoon kosher salt**
**1 bunch fresh spinach, roughly chopped**
**1 cup mayonnaise**
**4 ounces goat cheese**
**4 ounces Parmesan cheese**
**4 ounces mozzarella cheese**
**1 tablespoon minced garlic**
**2 green onions, thinly sliced**
**1 teaspoon dry crushed red pepper**
**1 bunch fresh basil**
**2 eggs**
**½ cup all-purpose flour**
**1 cup cornmeal**
**1 cup buttermilk**

Cut tomatoes into ½-inch-thick slices; place on a paper-towel-lined rack, sprinkle with salt and let sit 20 minutes before patting dry with paper towel. Preheat oven to 375°. In a mixing bowl, stir together spinach, mayonnaise, cheeses, garlic, green onion and red pepper. Spread a fourth of spinach mixture in bottom of a prepared glass pie dish. Top with half of tomato slices, then basil and half of remaining spinach mixture. Repeat layers once and cover loosely with foil. Bake 30 minutes. In a bowl, stir together remaining ingredients, uncover pie and pour over top. Bake 20 to 25 minutes more or until golden brown and set. Set aside 10 to 15 minutes before serving.

**Restaurant Recipe**

# The Gamekeeper Restaurant & Bar

**3005 Shulls Mill Road**
**Boone, NC 28607**
**828-963-7400**
**www.gamekeeper-nc.com**
**Find us on Facebook & Instagram**

The Gamekeeper Restaurant & Bar is well known for its interesting and delicious interpretations of Southern classics. As one of the first restaurants in the area to embrace a farm-to-table model, only the freshest of local ingredients and humanely farm-raised meats are served. The menu changes seasonally, blending the traditional with the exotic, satisfying both meat and veggie lovers. The Gamekeeper is nestled in the beautiful Blue Ridge Mountains, in a stone cottage just two miles off the Blue Ridge Parkway. It is the ultimate marriage of fine dining and comfort food and a must-visit while in the Mountains Region.

Summer:
**Wednesday – Sunday: 5:00 pm to 9:00 pm**
Winter:
**Thursday – Saturday: 5:00 pm to 9:00 pm**

## *Chow Chow*

**1 head red cabbage, chopped**
**3 tablespoons chopped garlic**
**1 onion, chopped**
**2 ounces apple cider vinegar**
**½ teaspoon curry powder**
**1 pinch cumin**
**2 tablespoons hot sauce**
**Salt and pepper to taste**

In a saucepan over medium-high heat, add cabbage, garlic and onion; sauté until tender. Add vinegar, curry powder, cumin and hot sauce. Pulse mixture in a food processor until well combined. Season to taste with salt and pepper.

**Restaurant Recipe**

## *Blueberry Cobbler*

### *Batter:*

**2 cups all-purpose flour**
**2 teaspoons baking powder**
**½ cup sugar**
**1 egg**
**½ cup milk**
**½ teaspoon vanilla extract**
**1 lemon, zested and juiced**

Mix all ingredients together in a bowl, reserving lemon juice for Cobbler mixture; set aside.

### *Cobbler:*

**4 cups washed blueberries**
**1 cup sugar**
**Reserved lemon juice**
**Splash kirsch**
**Splash Grand Marnier**
**Splash peach brandy**
**2 tablespoons cornstarch**
**Vanilla ice cream and fresh peach, for serving**

Preheat oven to 350°. In a bowl, stir together remaining ingredients; transfer mixture to a 9- to 10-inch casserole dish. Pour batter over top. Bake until golden brown. Serve with vanilla ice cream and a sliced fresh peach.

**Restaurant Recipe**

**345 Hardin Street**
**Boone, NC 28607**
**828-268-9900**
**www.stickboybread.com • Find us on Facebook**

Situated on Hardin Street, across from the campus of Appalachian State, is Stick Boy Bread Company. Hardin Street is the original Stick Boy location, where it has been sharing a love of great food with High Country since 2001. Using traditional ingredients and methods, Stick Boy bakers produce a wide range of baked goods. There is also a full espresso and smoothie bar. Stick Boy Bread Company may be small, but in this bustling production bakery, you'll find naturally fermented sourdough loaves, chocolate tortes, cream cheese cinnamon rolls, delicious frothy cappuccinos, and so much more.

**Monday – Friday: 7:00 am to 6:30 pm**
**Saturday: 7:00 am to 5:30 pm**

## *Pumpkin Walnut Bread*

**7 cups all-purpose flour**
**4 cups sugar**
**5 tablespoons pumpkin spice mix**
**1 tablespoon salt**
**1 teaspoon baking powder**
**2 cups walnut pieces**
**1 cup raisins**
**1½ (15-ounce) cans pumpkin**
**1¼ cups melted butter**
**8 eggs, whisked**
**2 tablespoons milk**
**2 tablespoons oil**
**2 tablespoons water**
**1 teaspoon vanilla**

Preheat oven to 350°. In large bowl, mix all ingredients until well combined. Split batter between 8 greaased and floured loaf pans, each scaled to 550 grams. Bake 45 minutes. Pumpkin Walnut Bread is done when a toothpick inserted into center comes out clean.

**Restaurant Recipe**

## *Spring Green Smoothie*

**1¼ cups orange juice**
**Handful fresh spinach**
**½ cup each chopped frozen mango, banana and peaches**

Add ingredients to blender in order. Blend until smooth and enjoy this healthy, refreshing treat. Yields 1 (16-ounce) Spring Green Smoothie.

**Restaurant Recipe**

**211 Boone Heights Drive**
**Boone, NC 28607**
**828-265-4141**
**www.stickboybread.com • Find us on Facebook**

After years of customers asking for sandwiches and grumbling about parking and seating, Stick Boy Bread Company opened Stick Boy Kitchen, simply known as "the Kitchen" among locals. They finally have it all! Opened in 2013, the Kitchen is a café that offers breakfast plates, bagels, homemade soups, scrumptious sandwiches, and fresh salads, all made with the same singular focus on quality ingredients, freshness, and creativity for which Stick Boy has come to be known. If you are looking for baked goods, coffee, espresso, or smoothies, the Kitchen has everything you're craving. Stop by and get some real food.

**Monday – Saturday: 7:00 am to 8:00 pm**

## *Tomato Basil Soup*

**¼ cup chopped white onion**
**2 tablespoons olive oil**
**10 cloves garlic, minced**
**½ teaspoon salt**
**¼ teaspoon pepper**
**2½ cups tomato paste**
**2½ cups fire-roasted tomatoes**
**4 cups warmed heavy cream**
**3 tablespoons vegetable base**
**½ teaspoon baking soda**
**½ teaspoon sugar**
**1¾ cup basil leaves**
**6 tablespoons grated Parmesan cheese**

In a saucepan over medium heat, sauté onion in oil about 10 minutes. Add garlic and spices; cook until fragrant. Transfer mixture to a stock pot; stir in tomato paste and tomatoes. Add 2½ cups water and remaining ingredients, except cheese; bring to a simmer and puree with an immersion blender until smooth. Add Parmesan. Taste and adjust seasonings, if necessary. Serves 15 to 20.

**Restaurant Recipe**

## *Chicken Salad*

*Just 11 simple ingredients the whole family will enjoy. Try this next to our Tomato Basil Soup.*

**3 chicken breasts, cooked and diced**
**3 chicken thighs, cooked and shredded**
**2 tablespoons diced red onion**
**½ cup diced cranberries**
**1 stalk celery, diced**
**2 teaspoons spicy brown mustard**
**¼ cup mayonnaise**
**1½ teaspoons cider vinegar**
**½ teaspoon salt**
**1 pinch pepper**
**1 pinch garlic powder**

In a bowl, mix all ingredients until evenly distributed; refrigerate at least 1 hour. Enjoy on fresh-baked yeast slider rolls, layered with crisp lettuce. Serves 6 to 8.

**Restaurant Recipe**

## Mayberry's Soups & Sandwiches

**30 West Main Street**
**Brevard, NC 28712**
**828-862-8646**
**www.mayberrys.co • Find us on Facebook**

Mayberry's isn't the town where Andy Griffith grew up, nor is it where the television show was filmed. However, just like Andy Griffith's Mayberry, Mayberry's Soups & Sandwiches is a simple place where people are important. From the beginning, the goal was to establish Mayberry's as a comfortable place where customers from all walks of life could gather for simple food and good company. Choose from a menu of soups, sandwiches, sauces, and dinner entrees that are all made in house, using original recipes. You can also enjoy a selection of wine and beer while you dine. Ask about the special homemade sauces and limited specialty drinks.

**Monday – Thursday: 11:00 am to 9:00 pm**
**Friday & Saturday: 8:00 am to 9:00 pm**
**Sunday: 8:00 am to 3:00 pm**

### *Dill Turkey*

**1 (3½-pound) turkey breast, halved**
**¼ cup freshly chopped dill weed**
**1 cup dill relish**
**½ to 1 cup mayonnaise**
**¼ cup minced celery**

Chop half of turkey; add to a large bowl. Lightly process other half of turkey in a food processor; add to bowl. Add dill weed, celery, relish and mayonnaise. Mix all ingredients until combined. Serve.

**Restaurant Recipe**

## Turkey & Thyme Pot Pie

**4 cups turkey broth**
**2½ tablespoons thyme**
**1 pint whipping cream**
**¾ to 1 cup all-purpose flour**
**2 pounds turkey, shredded**
**1 to 2 cups green peas**
**2 to 3 carrots, diced and cooked soft**

In a saucepan over medium-high heat, bring broth to a boil. Add thyme and ½ cup water. In a bowl, mix cream and flour; add to broth. Adjust water content as needed for thickness. Add turkey, peas and carrots to broth mixture and stir. Pour filling into a glass pie dish; set aside.

### Crust

**1½ cups self-rising flour**
**1½ cups buttermilk**
**¾ cup melted butter**
**Thyme for sprinkling**

Preheat oven to 375°. In a bowl, mix flour and buttermilk. Stir in butter. Pour batter over pie filling. Sprinkle with thyme. Bake 45 to 60 minutes or until crust is golden brown.

**Restaurant Recipe**

## Chicken Cordon Bleu Soup

**¼ cup butter**
**¼ cup flour**
**2½ cups half-and-half**
**2½ cups whole milk**
**2 cups chicken stock**
**1 (8-ounce) package cream cheese, cubed**
**2 cups cubed chicken**
**1½ cups cubed ham**
**¼ cup cooked, crumbled bacon**
**1½ cups water**
**2 cups shredded Swiss cheese**

In a saucepan over very low heat, melt butter; add flour and cook 1 minute, stirring constantly. Stir in milk, half-and-half and chicken broth. Keep an eye on soup; stir constantly, as cream will separate if overheated. Stir in cream cheese until smooth. Bring mixture to a heavy simmer; stir in ham, chicken and bacon. Stir in 1½ cups water. Remove from heat, add Swiss cheese and serve.

**Restaurant Recipe**

# Doc Brown's BBQ

**1320 Smokey Park Highway**
**Candler, NC 28715**
**828-633-6901**
**www.docbrownbbq.com • Find us on Facebook**

Doc Brown's BBQ is a family-owned barbecue restaurant and food truck intent on serving the best barbecue in the land. Specializing in all things pig, the barbecue joint is known to cook a mean chicken salad and barbecue tempeh. Best of all, the 'cue is wood-smoked. Doc Brown's also whips up sides reminiscent of your grandmother's Southern cuisine. Don't miss the mac and cheese or the church picnic potato salad. And with a selection of different barbecue sauces, from Eastern Carolina to Alabama White, you can tailor your meal to your taste every single time. Visit Doc Brown's BBQ for tried-and-true family recipes that will have you in hog heaven.

**Tuesday – Saturday: 11:00 am to 8:00 pm**
**Sunday: Noon to 4:00 pm**

## *Cucumber & Tomato Salad*

**8 cups peeled, diced cucumber**
**8 cups coarsely chopped tomato**
**12 green onions, chopped**
**2 cups sugar**
**1 cup white vinegar**
**1 cup red wine vinegar**
**Salt and pepper to taste**

Add vegetables to a bowl. In another bowl, mix sugar, vinegars and ½ cup water until sugar dissolves; pour over vegetables, toss and adjust to taste with salt and pepper. Chill overnight before serving.

**Restaurant Recipe**

## *Mac & Cheese*

**1 stick butter**
**4 tablespoons flour**
**2 (12.5-ounce) cans evaporated milk**
**2 eggs, beaten**
**Salt and black pepper to taste**
**4 cups grated sharp Cheddar cheese, divided**
**16 ounces elbow macaroni, cooked and drained**

Preheat oven to 375°. In a saucepan over medium heat, melt butter; gradually add flour. Cook, stirring constantly, until golden brown. Add milk; cook, stirring often, until thickened. Remove from heat and temper eggs into mixture. Adjust seasoning to taste with salt and pepper. In a large casserole dish, toss together 3 cups Cheddar cheese, macaroni, salt and pepper; pour cheese sauce over top and mix thoroughly. Top with remaining Cheddar. Bake 50 minutes or until browned. Rest 15 minutes before serving.

**Restaurant Recipe**

# Winslow's Hideaway

**Village Walk Way**
**At the Crossroads Highway 107 South**
**Cashiers, NC 28717**
**828-743-2226**
**www.winslowshideawaync.com**
**Find us on Facebook**

Winslow's Hideaway is the premier American cuisine restaurant in the Cashiers, Highlands, and Lake Toxaway areas. This intimate 38-seat restaurant is family-owned and -operated. Boasting forty-five years of experience, Chef Winslow Jones has created recipes featured in *Bon Appétit* magazine and 100 Favorite Restaurant Recipes, as well as various other publications. Chef Winslow's classic creations center around the finest, dry-aged prime steaks and chops; fresh seafood, including local mountain trout and fresh blue crab; original recipe soups; and decadent desserts. Complementing the inspired fare, outstanding service is headed up by the chef's son, Edgar, and his wife, Terri. Edgar oversees the award-winning wine list and full-service bar, while Terri is responsible for the restaurant's cozy atmosphere and decoration.

**Tuesday – Saturday: 5:00 pm to 9:00 pm**

## *Sabayon Cream with Strawberries & Blueberries*

**1 quart heavy whipping cream**
**½ cup powdered sugar**
**8 tablespoons brandy, rum or Marsala wine, divided**
**6 egg yolks**
**6 tablespoons granulated sugar**
**1 pint strawberries, wash and sliced**
**1 pint blueberries, washed**
**Fresh mint leaves for garnish**

In a stand mixer, whip heavy cream, powdered sugar and 2 tablespoons liquor until peaks develop; refrigerate whipped cream. Bring double-boiler to a boil; add egg yolks, granulated sugar and remaining liquor, whisking until thickened—do not overcook. Transfer pan to ice bath, continuing to whisk; refrigerate 10 minutes. Fold half whipped cream into egg mixture until blended into Sabayon Cream. Toss together 1½ cups each strawberries and blueberries; divide between 8 dessert glasses. Divide Sabayon Cream between glasses, then top with remaining whipped cream and remaining berries. Garnish with mint leaves.

**Restaurant Recipe**

## *Trout Winslow*

**5 cups tarragon vinegar**

**2 tablespoons coarse ground black pepper**

**2 yellow onions, sliced**

**¼ cup finely chopped parsley plus more for garnish**

**6 cups melted butter, divided**

**6 egg yolks**

**8 (8- to 10-ounce) trout fillets or (12- to 14-ounce) boneless whole trout**

**Flour for dusting**

**Salt, pepper and paprika to taste**

**2 pounds fresh jumbo lump blue crabmeat**

**Lemon wedges for garnish**

In a skillet over medium heat, cook vinegar, black pepper, onions and ¼ cup parsley until vinegar is reduced by two-thirds and onions are translucent; transfer reduction to a blender and purée until smooth. In a saucepan, bring 3 cups butter and 6 to 8 heaping tablespoons purée to a bubbling simmer; cool. Purée yolks in blender while lightly streaming in cooled mixture to make béarnaise sauce; transfer to bowl and set aside. Preheat oven to 325°. Dust trout skins with flour; place skin side down on 2 baking sheets covered with 1 cup melted butter each. Sprinkle with salt, pepper and paprika; bake 8 to 10 minutes or until flaky. In a skillet over medium heat, lightly toss remaining butter and crab, taking care not to break crab. Place trout on warmed plates and top with equal amounts strained hot crab. Spoon 2 to 3 tablespoons béarnaise over each plate, then garnish with additional paprika and parsley. Serve with lemon wedges.

**Restaurant Recipe**

**219 Old Main Street**
**Cliffside, NC 28024**
**828-657-0049**
**www.dutchbroadatcliffside.com**
**Find us on Facebook**

Named after the owner's heritage and its location on the Broad River, The Dutch Broad Café unites farm-grown vegetables and humanely, locally raised meats with creative culinary skills. The Café harbors great love and respect for the land and its preservation, focusing on farm-fresh, organic, regionally grown dishes. Dutch Broad sources its ingredients from White Turtle Farm, a modern family farm using sustainable and organic small-scale practices. The Café's food is beautifully presented, deeply flavored, and simply delicious.

**Daily: 11:00 am to 2:00 pm**

## *Dutchees ("Bitterballen")*

**¼ cup butter**
**¼ cup flour**
**1½ cups milk**
**2 cups grated Old Amsterdam cheese**
**2 tablespoons chopped roasted red pepper**
**Pinch salt and pepper**
**2 eggs**
**1 cup breadcrumbs**
**Oil for frying**
**Marinara sauce**
**Finely minced parsley for garnish**

In a saucepan, melt butter; stir in flour, then slowly add milk until a smooth, thick sauce forms. Bring to a boil and stir 1 minute. Remove from heat and stir in cheese, red pepper, salt and pepper; transfer mixture to a bowl and refrigerate several hours until set. Beat together eggs with 1 tablespoon water in one bowl and place breadcrumbs in another bowl. In a large saucepan, heat several inches oil to 350°. Remove batter from refrigerator, scoop out tablespoonfuls and roll into balls. Dip into egg mixture and roll in breadcrumbs; repeat once to make sure balls are fully coated. Drop Dutchees into hot oil; fry 2 minutes or until golden and heated through, then drain on paper towels. Plate marinara, top with Dutchees and garnish with parsley.

**Restaurant Recipe**

## *Flash-Fried Shrimp with Spicy Aioli*

*Spicy Aioli:*

**1 cup mayonnaise**
**3 tablespoons hot sauce**
**1 cup Thai sweet chili sauce**
**2 teaspoons rice wine vinegar**

In a bowl, mix all ingredients until combined. Pour into a squeeze bottle and store in refrigerator while preparing shrimp.

*Shrimp:*

**Oil for frying**
**1 cup cornstarch**
**4 large eggs**
**1 cup flour**
**1 cup panko breadcrumbs**
**2 teaspoons kosher salt**
**½ teaspoon each black pepper, onion powder and garlic powder**
**2 pounds large shrimp, peeled, deveined and tails left on**
**½ cup freshly minced parsley**

Heat several inches oil in a saucepan to 350°. In a bowl, add cornstarch; in another bowl, beat eggs with 1 tablespoon water; and in a third bowl, whisk together flour, breadcrumbs, salt, pepper and powders. Dredge shrimp in cornstarch, dip into egg mixture and coat in breadcrumb mixture. Drop shrimp in hot oil, frying 2 to 3 minutes or until golden brown. Drain on paper towels, then arrange on a plate. Drizzle with prepared Spicy Aioli and garnish with parsley.

**Restaurant Recipe**

# Jonny Mac's Lowcountry Grille & BBQ

**3885 Hendersonville Road**
**Fletcher, NC 28732**
**828-376-3679**
**www.jonnymacsnc.com • Find us on Facebook**

Welcome to Jonny Mac's Lowcountry Grille & BBQ, where you'll discover the taste of the Lowcountry as well as delicious barbecue. Let your taste buds pack a suitcase for a tour of Lowcountry-Cajun fusion. Jonny has combined his favorite flavors from his travels and experiences working with great chefs in Charleston and New Orleans. To top it off, he also serves great-tasting barbecue cooked according to western North Carolina tradition. Bring your appetite and a hankering for tasty, fresh-made food on down to Jonny Mac's.

**Monday – Saturday: 11:00 am to 9:00 pm**
**Sunday: 11:00 am to 3:00 pm**

## *Jambalaya*

**2 onions, diced**
**4 green bell peppers, diced**
**3 stalks celery, diced**
**1 tablespoon minced garlic**
**4 tablespoons vegetable oil**
**1 cup Italian seasoning**
**3 tablespoons Cajun seasoning**
**1½ cup Worcestershire sauce**
**5 bay leaves**
**5 (14.5-ounce) cans diced tomatoes**
**1 tablespoon chicken base**
**2 pounds raw andouille sausage, chunked**
**2 pounds boneless chicken, chunked**
**Cornstarch to thicken**

Sauté onions, peppers, celery and garlic in oil with seasonings, Worcestershire and bay leaves until onions are translucent. Stir in tomatoes, chicken base and 1½ quarts water; bring to a boil. Add sausage and chicken; simmer until both are done. Stir in cornstarch as needed to thicken.

**Restaurant Recipe**

## *Mac's BBBB (Bacon-and-Beef Baked Beans)*

**1 pound ground beef**
**1 cup chopped Vidalia onion**
**1 pound bacon**
**2 (15-ounce) cans pork and beans**
**2 (15.25-ounce) cans lima beans**
**2 (15-ounce) cans pinto beans**
**2 (15-ounce) cans kidney beans**
**½ cup ketchup**
**1 tablespoon mustard**
**¾ cup packed brown sugar**
**1 tablespoon vinegar**

In a skillet over medium-high heat, brown beef and sauté onion; drain fat. In another skillet, cook bacon until crisp; crumble and add to beef and onion. In a large bowl, mix beef mixture and remaining ingredients. Transfer to a 9x13-inch baking dish. Bake at 325° for 1 hour.

**Restaurant Recipe**

# The Copper Door

**2 Sullivan Street**
**Hayesville, NC 28904**
**828-389-8460**
**www.thecopperdoor.com • Find us on Facebook**

Acclaimed by critics and guests alike, The Copper Door features dry-aged steaks, fresh seafood, and a well-chosen selection of quality wines. The restaurant received Wine Spectator's Award of Excellence and was named one of OpenTable's Top 100 Restaurants in the country. The menu offers a variety of delicious entrees, from scallops casino to roast rack of lamb. Start your meal with an outstanding appetizer, a hearty soup, or fresh salad. Finish with chocolate decadence or bananas Foster for an especially sweet ending. The Copper Door offers guests a warm, inviting dining room, a romantic patio with a courtyard, and a full bar.

**Tuesday – Saturday: 5:00 pm to 10:00 pm**

**Reservations Recommended**

## *Glazed Carrots*

**2 tablespoons cooking oil**

**½ yellow onion, peeled and julienned**

**2 cups fresh carrots, peeled and chopped into bite-size pieces**

**1 teaspoon brown sugar**

**1 teaspoon Chef Paul Prudhomme's Blackened Redfish Magic seasoning**

**Salt and pepper to taste**

Heat oil in a pan over medium-high heat until it begins to smoke. Add onion; cook until caramelization begins. Add carrots, sugar and spices; stir until well coated. Reduce heat to low, cover with a tight-fitting lid and cook 12 to 15 minutes or until just tender. Once carrots are just tender, adjust seasoning to taste and serve. If there is a lot of liquid in pan, cook uncovered over medium-high heat until liquid is reduced to a glaze, then serve.

**Restaurant Recipe**

## *Honey Lavender Dressing*

*Lavender Vinegar:*

**Fresh lavender sprigs**

**White balsamic vinegar**

Soak lavender in vinegar 2 days. Strain before use.

*Dressing:*

**3 eggs yolks**

**¼ cup prepared Lavender Vinegar**

**¼ cup honey**

**2 teaspoons vanilla extract**

**¾ cup olive oil**

**¾ cup vegetable oil**

Add all ingredients except oils to blender. Blend on high, carefully pouring oils into blender until dressing is fully emulsified.

**Restaurant Recipe**

**Award-Winning BBQ & Wood Oven Neapolitan Pizza!**

# Flat Rock Wood Room

**1501 Greenville Highway**
**Hendersonville, NC 28792**
**828-435-1391**
**www.flatrockwoodroom.com • Find us on Facebook**

Flat Rock Wood Room prepares award-winning barbecue and wood-fired gourmet pizzas. With a state-of-the-art smoker, the restaurant smokes pork, brisket, and chicken to create appetizing sandwiches, pulled pork platters, rib platters, half-chicken platters, and more. The restaurant also uses a Neapolitan pizza oven to create flavorful wood-fired pizzas that are sure to please even the most discriminating taste buds. Every entree comes with sweet cornbread with honey-pecan butter and two tasty sides of your choice. Try barbecue baked beans, apple slaw, potato salad, collard greens, beer-battered steak fries, sweet potato fries, onion straws, cheese and bacon grits, or French green onions. Let Flat Rock Wood Room prepare your next meal.

**Wednesday, Thursday & Sunday: 11:30 am to 8:00 pm**
**Friday & Saturday: 11:30 am to 9:00 pm**

## *Okinawa BBQ Chicken*

**2 pounds bone-in chicken thighs**
**1 cup soy sauce**
**1 tablespoon ground ginger**
**2 tablespoons chopped fresh cilantro**
**2 cloves garlic, minced**
**½ lemon, juiced**
**Kosher salt and freshly ground black pepper to taste**
**2 tablespoons butter**
**2 tablespoons extra virgin olive oil**
**½ cup honey**
**Sesame seeds for garnish**
**2 whole green onions**
**1 cup fried rice**

Rinse and pat dry chicken; place in a shallow dish. Add soy sauce, ginger, cilantro, garlic and lemon juice. Toss chicken to coat; refrigerate, covered, allowing to marinate 3 to 4 hours. Remove chicken from marinade and season with salt and pepper. In a large skillet over medium-high heat, melt butter in olive oil. When butter stops foaming, add honey and chicken thighs, frying 2 minutes on each side or until browned. As glaze reduces, continue turning chicken in skillet to coat; cook until sticky but not cooked through. Finish thighs on an open-flame barbecue grill for best flavor. Garnish with sesame seeds and green onions; serve over fried rice.

**Restaurant Recipe**

## *Pisgah Pork Potato Skins*

**Olive oil for seasoning**
**4 Idaho baking potatoes, washed**
**Coarse salt for seasoning**
**4 cups barbecued pulled pork, divided**
**1 cup shredded mozzarella cheese**
**Barbecue sauce for topping**
**Sour cream for topping**
**Salt and pepper to taste**
**Chopped green onions for garnish**

Preheat oven to 350°. Oil potatoes and rub with coarse salt; poke a couple holes in each with a knife, then wrap in foil and place on baking sheet. Bake potatoes 1 to 2 hours or until tender; remove from oven, cut in half lengthwise and scoop out centers, taking care not to break through skin. Fill each skin with ½ cup pulled pork and sprinkle with mozzarella; return to oven for 15 minutes. When done, top with a drizzle of barbecue sauce, a spoonful of sour cream, and salt and pepper to taste. Garnish with green onions. Serve.

**Restaurant Recipe**

# Harvey's at The Henderson

201 3rd Avenue West
Hendersonville, NC 28739
828-696-2001
www.thehendersonnc.com
Find us on Facebook

Nestled inside The Henderson Inn's cozy walls is Harvey's, a restaurant and bar, which serves delicious food, prepared by an award-winning chef, to guests and walk-ins alike. You will enjoy a diverse menu of small plates, which are delivered to you, spontaneously, the moment they are created. The dishes are as varied as the ingredients they are prepared from, but all are served in exquisite fashion and meant to be savored. Stop by for a gourmet breakfast on Sunday mornings, followed by a gorgeous brunch that stretches into the afternoon. Whether you stay overnight or just drop in for a drink, the team at Harvey's can't wait to welcome you.

**Thursday – Saturday: 5:00 pm to 9:00 pm**
**Sunday Brunch: 10:30 am to 2:30 pm**

## *The Henderson Caprese with Cilantro Dressing*

### *Cilantro Dressing:*

**1 bunch cilantro, stems and leaves**
**1 jalapeño, deseeded**
**1 cup rice wine vinegar**
**½ cup vegetable stock**
**2 cups grape seed oil**
**2 tablespoons salt**

Place all ingredients in a food processor and blend until cilantro is integrated. Strain through a fine-meshed conical strainer; discard trappings. Set Dressing aside.

### *Caprese:*

**4 tablespoons balsamic reduction**
**4 cherry tomatoes**
**1 ball buffalo mozzarella**
**1 teaspoon cilantro leaves**
**2 tablespoons Cilantro Dressing**
**1 teaspoon Maldon salt**

Spoon balsamic reduction into a squeeze bottle; squeeze 4 lines balsamic reduction across a square plate, in a tic-tac-toe formation. Slice tomatoes and mozzarella in half or quarters, depending on size. Place one piece tomato or mozzarella in each of outer squares. Place a cilantro leaf on each mozzarella piece. Spoon Cilantro Dressing in center square. Sprinkle everything with salt and serve immediately.

Restaurant Recipe

## Baked Crab Cakes with Chipotle Aioli

### *Mustard Aioli:*

**2 eggs**
**2 tablespoons Dijon mustard**
**2 tablespoons whole-grain mustard**
**1 lemon, juiced**
**2 cups canola oil**
**Salt and pepper to taste**

In a food processor, blend mustards and lemon juice. Process oil in until smooth. Add salt and pepper.

### *Crab Cakes:*

**1 (16-ounce) can jumbo lump crabmeat**
**1 each red and yellow bell pepper, finely diced**
**1 ear corn, blanched, grilled and sliced from cob**
**1 lemon, juiced**
**1 cup prepared Mustard Aioli**
**1 bunch chives, finely diced**
**Salt and pepper to taste**
**Panko breadcrumbs to cover**

In a large bowl, gently fold together all ingredients except salt, pepper and panko without overmixing. Season with salt and pepper. Using a 2.75-inch ring mold, cover bottom of mold with panko; pack crab mixture in, forming a tight patty. Top patty with panko. Remove from mold and place on a parchment-lined baking sheet. Repeat for 12 crab cakes; refrigerate 30 minutes. Bake at 350° for 25 minutes until panko is browned, flipping halfway through.

### *Chipotle Aioli:*

**2 eggs**
**½ (12-ounce) can chipotles in adobo sauce**
**½ shallot, finely diced**
**1 teaspoon grated ginger**
**2 cups canola oil**
**1 lemon, juiced**
**2 tablespoons cilantro, finely chopped**

Blend eggs, chipotles, shallot and ginger in a food processor until a paste forms. Process oil in until emulsified. Stir in lemon juice and cilantro.

Restaurant Recipe

# Smoky Mountain Diner

**70 Lance Avenue**
**Hot Springs, NC 28743**
**828-622-7571**
**Find us on Facebook**

Smoky Mountain Diner began as a textile manufacturing plant, the Dogwood Mill, in 1944. In the sixties, it became a tomato packing plant and, later, a skating rink. In the eighties, the building was converted into a restaurant. Genia Peterson bought the restaurant in the nineties, trading a career in hospice care for hospitality. She soon learned it takes a village to run a restaurant. In fact, her family serves a vital role in helping out. Don't forget to try Genia's pinto beans and homemade pepper relish, made from a recipe handed down through generations. Come visit for tasty food and friendly service that will make you feel like family.

**Monday – Thursday: 6:00 am to 8:00 pm**
**Friday & Saturday: 6:30 am to 8:00 pm**

## *Pepper Relish*

**2 cups dried pepper flakes**
**2 large onions, diced**
**2 cups vinegar**
**2 cups sugar**
**Salt to taste**
**2 tablespoons ground cinnamon**

Add all ingredients to a large stockpot over high heat; bring to a boil. Cook 10 minutes. Carefully transfer mixture to half-pint jars and seal.

**Restaurant Recipe**

## *Squash Casserole*

**½ teaspoon salt**
**1 pound yellow squash, diced**
**1 medium onion, sliced**
**½ stick margarine, melted**
**1 (10.5-ounce) can cream of mushroom soup**
**¼ pound breadcrumbs**

In a large stockpot over high heat, add enough water to cover vegetables. Add salt and bring to a boil; add squash and onion, cooking until tender. Carefully drain water and mash vegetables. Stir in margarine, soup and most of breadcrumbs. Transfer mixture to a buttered 9x13-inch casserole dish; sprinkle top with remaining breadcrumbs. Bake at 375° for 20 minutes.

**Restaurant Recipe**

**14535 Highway 209**
**Hot Springs, NC 28743**
**828-622-7400**
**www.trustgeneralstore.com • Find us on Facebook & Instagram: @trustgeneralstoreandcafe**

Trust General Store & Café is a must-stop on your next visit to the Mountains Region. Surrounded by unspoiled, rugged mountain ranges and pristine streams, the charming setting and gracious Southern hospitality will make you feel like you've stepped back in time. Housed in an early-1900s-era building, Trust General Store & Café has been in operation since 2008 and keeps with the tradition of friendly service for which previous general stores in the area were known. Stop by the café for hearty portions of home-style country favorites, like fried pickles, fried chicken, macaroni and cheese, meatloaf, and so much more. Trust General's food will make you feel good.

**Café Hours:**
**Thursday – Saturday: 11:00 am to 7:00 pm**
**Sunday: 11:00 am to 4:00 pm**

## *Reese's Peanut Butter Cake*

**1 box dark chocolate cake mix plus ingredients to prepare**

**2 cups powdered sugar**

**½ cup creamy peanut butter**

**1½ teaspoons vanilla extract**

**¼ cup milk**

**1 (12-ounce) package semisweet chocolate chips**

**6 to 8 peanut butter cups, chilled and chopped**

Prepare cake according to package directions; cool. In a bowl, mix powdered sugar, peanut butter and vanilla. Add milk a little at a time, mixing well after each addition, until a buttercream icing texture is achieved; spread peanut butter frosting evenly over cooled cake. Melt chocolate chips in a microwave-safe bowl 1 minute, stirring until smooth. Spread chocolate over peanut butter frosting. Sprinkle chopped peanut butter cups over warm chocolate; chill to set. Bring to room temperature before cutting.

**Restaurant Recipe**

## *Famous Hot Fudge Cake*

**1 box chocolate cake mix plus ingredients to prepare**

**Hot fudge sauce for topping**

**Vanilla ice cream for topping**

Prepare cake according to package directions for a 9x13-inch pan; cool and cut into slices. Plate slice and top with fudge sauce. Microwave 10 seconds, then top with vanilla ice cream.

**Restaurant Recipe**

# Larkin's on the Lake

**1020 Memorial Highway**
**Lake Lure, NC 28746**
**828-625-4075**
**www.larkinsonthelake.com**
**Find us on Facebook**

In 1998, Mark and Larkin Hammond established Larkin's on the Lake. This premier dining destination offers the only lake-front dining experience available on the beautiful Lake Lure. The restaurant even features a dock so that customers on the lake can dock their boats and enjoy a delicious meal. Downstairs, the Bayfront Bar & Grill serves lunch and dinner, offering indoor and outdoor seating. As evening approaches, the upstairs dining room opens, serving dinner entrees, while the Bayfront Bar & Grill continues to serve burgers, sandwiches, and dinner entrees downstairs. Larkin's also boasts a full bar, featuring eight draft beers, bottled beers, and wines. "Drive, boat, or swim... just get here!"

**Downstairs:**
**Sunday – Thursday: 11:30 am to 9:00 pm**
**Friday & Saturday: 11:30 am to 9:30 pm**
**Upstairs:**
**Sunday – Thursday: 5:00 pm to 9:00 pm**
**Friday & Saturday: 5:00 pm to 9:30 pm**

*Call for Seasonal Hours*

# Chicken Tortilla Soup

**3 quarts chicken broth**
**2 teaspoons ground cumin**
**2 teaspoons chili powder**
**2 teaspoons dried oregano**
**15 ounces canned black beans, drained and rinse**
**15 ounces canned whole-kernel corn, drained**
**2 pounds cooked, boneless, skinless chicken breasts, finely chopped**
**2 cups fresh pico de gallo**
**2 cups chopped fresh cilantro**
**Cheddar cheese to taste**
**Tortilla strips to taste**

In a large stockpot, add chicken broth, cumin, chili powder and oregano; bring to a boil. Add beans, corn, chicken and pico de gallo; reduce heat to low and simmer, stirring occasionally, about 10 minutes. To serve, ladle soup into bowls, add cilantro and garnish with cheese and tortilla strips. Enjoy.

**Restaurant Recipe**

# Crab Nachos

**4 cups back fin crabmeat**
**4 cups claw crabmeat**
**1 cup chopped red bell pepper**
**1 cup chopped red onion**
**½ cup plus 2 tablespoons whole grain mustard**
**1¼ cup mayonnaise**
**1 bunch chopped parsley**
**¼ cup crab base**
**1 tablespoon lobster base**
**1 tablespoon Old Bay seasoning**
**1 dash salt and pepper**
**Tortilla chips to taste**
**Pico de gallo to taste**
**Queso to taste**
**Shredded lettuce to taste**
**1 lemon, sliced into wedges**

In a large bowl, gently fold together all ingredients except chips, pico de gallo, queso, lettuce and lemon. Arrange a bed of chips on a plate; top with crab mixture, pico de gallo and queso. Serve with shredded lettuce and a lemon wedge. Enjoy.

**Restaurant Recipe**

# Luna Del Sol

**143 Whitney Boulevard**
**Lake Lure, NC 28746**
**828-625-2007**
**Find us on Facebook**

Welcome to Luna Del Sol, a culinary gem located in Lake Lure. This top-rated eatery offers a wonderful menu, an extensive bar, and a buzzing atmosphere. Enjoy buffalo wings, soups, salads, a variety of pastas, pork chops, fish, burgers, subs, gourmet pizzas, and more, each artfully prepared to please your every taste. Cap your meal with your drink of choice, and it's a party for your taste buds. Stop by Luna Del Sol today.

**Wednesday – Sunday: 5:00 pm to 9:00 pm**

## Freckle-Faced Taters

**2 large baked potatoes**
**¼ cup grated Cheddar cheese**
**4 tablespoons melted butter**
**2 tablespoons milk**
**¼ teaspoon hot sauce**
**⅛ teaspoon salt**
**1 teaspoon Worcestershire sauce**
**½ cup crushed croutons**

Set oven to broil. Quarter potatoes and place in baking dish. Sprinkle with cheese. In a small bowl, combine remaining ingredients. Pour over potatoes. Broil until browned.

**Local Favorite**

## Chicken & Tortilla Dumplings

**1 (2.5-pound) chicken**
**1 (8-count) package flour tortillas**
**½ cup butter**
**Salt and pepper to taste**
**2 tablespoons flour**
**½ cup milk**

Rinse chicken and place in Dutch oven; add water to cover and cook until tender. Remove chicken, reserving broth. Debone chicken and shred; set aside. Cut tortillas into bite-size pieces. Bring reserved broth to boil; add butter, salt and pepper. Drop tortilla pieces in broth and cook until tender. Add chicken back to pot. Blend flour and milk in small bowl and stir into broth to thicken, stirring constantly.

**Local Favorite**

# Buffalo Mercantile Company & Café

**6353 Buffalo Cove Road**
**Lenoir, NC 28645**
**828-758-9879**
**www.buffalomercantilecompany.com**
**Find us on Facebook**

The store began as a general store in 1897; Buffalo Mercantile Company operated in Buffalo Cove until 1924, when it was renamed Todd's Country Store and, thereafter, operated by the previous owners' daughter and son-in-law. Yet another purchase and name change later, in 2015, Buffalo Mercantile Company today features many upgrades and restorations for a new generation that celebrates the past while looking to the future. Enjoy Wi-Fi access, an expanded dining room, a deck, and stone patio with a fire pit and bridge over looking Corpening Branch. Shop more than 800 products or eat from a varied menu of salads, burgers, sandwiches, handmade pizzas, and more.

**Tuesday – Saturday: 11:00 am to 8:00 pm**
**Sunday: Noon to 6:00 pm**

## *Homemade Spicy Chili Beans*

**1½ pounds ground beef or turkey**
**1 (1.25-ounce) package chili seasoning**
**1 tablespoon ground cumin**
**1 (15-ounce) can black beans**
**1 (15-ounce) can kidney beans**
**1 (15-ounce can pinto beans**
**1 (10.75-ounce) can tomato purée**
**1 (14.5-ounce) can diced tomatoes**
**½ to ¾ bottle of V8 juice**
**Prepared cornbread or crackers, optional**
**Shredded Cheddar cheese for topping, optional**
**Sour cream for topping, optional**

In a skillet over medium-high heat, brown meat with chili seasoning and cumin; drain grease. In a large pot over medium heat, combine beans, purée, tomatoes and V8; stir in meat and cook until heated through, approximately 30 minutes. Serve with warm cornbread or crackers, shredded cheese and sour cream.

**Monthly Special Recipe**

## *Best Ever Chocolate Chip Cookies*

**3 cups flour**
**1 teaspoon baking soda**
**½ teaspoon baking powder**
**1 teaspoon salt**
**2 sticks butter, softened**
**1 cup sugar**
**1 cup packed brown sugar**
**2 teaspoons vanilla**
**2 eggs**
**2 cups Ghirardelli chocolate chips**

Preheat oven to 375°. In a bowl, combine flour, baking soda, baking powder and salt; set aside. In another bowl, cream together butter and sugars; beat in eggs and vanilla until fluffy. Mix in dry ingredients until just combined. Fold in chocolate chips until well combined. Drop tablespoon-size balls of dough onto a baking sheet lined with parchment. Bake 8 to 10 minutes until barely browned; remove from oven, rest 2 minutes and remove to a cooling rack.

**Restaurant Recipe**

# High Ridge Adventures Outfitting & BBQ

**4223 Highway 25-70**
**Marshall, NC 28753**
**828-649-9305**
**www.hrabbq.com • Find us on Facebook**

High Ridge Adventures Outfitting & BBQ is an outdoor trip planner, retail outlet, and restaurant serving real wood-smoked pit barbecue. With trip packages from fly fishing to wild turkey hunting, High Ridge Adventures has all the outdoor gear you'll need, sold by experienced guides and outfitters. They also know that no other style of cooking translates to the outdoors quite like barbecue. With their own rubs, sauces, and recipes, and using only the freshest ingredients, High Ridge Adventures is proud to serve some of the best barbecue in the Asheville area. From baby back ribs to brisket, High Ridge Adventures Outfitting & BBQ has something to suit every taste.

**Tuesday – Saturday: 10:30 am to 7:00 pm**

## Cheesy Potato Soup

**6 slices bacon**
**1 onion, chopped**
**2 pounds russet potatoes, peeled and chopped into ½-inch pieces**
**10 cloves garlic, minced**
**1 teaspoon salt**
**¼ teaspoon pepper**
**¼ cup all-purpose flour**
**2 cups milk**
**8 ounces Velveeta original cheese, sliced or chunked**
**1 cup shredded Cheddar cheese**
**1 tablespoon chopped fresh chives**

In a large pot over medium heat, cook bacon until crispy; drain on paper towels, cool and crumble. Add onion to bacon grease and cook until translucent, stirring occasionally. Add potatoes, garlic, salt and pepper; cook until garlic is fragrant, stirring frequently. Add flour and stir to incorporate. Stir in 2 cups water, milk and Velveeta; bring to a boil, then reduce to a simmer, allowing potatoes to cook and cheese to melt. Stir occasionally to prevent potatoes sticking. Serve topped with bacon, shredded Cheddar and chives.

Restaurant Recipe

## Smoked Pimento Cheese Spread

**3 cups shredded extra-sharp Cheddar cheese**
**1 cup shredded smoked mild Cheddar cheese**
**2 tablespoons finely diced roasted red pepper**
**½ cup plus 2 tablespoons mayonnaise**
**3 tablespoons sour cream**
**1 tablespoon spicy whole-grain mustard**
**1 tablespoon Texas Pete hot sauce**
**¼ teaspoon ground black pepper**
**¼ teaspoon herbes de Provence**
**⅛ teaspoon granulated garlic**
**⅛ teaspoon onion powder**

In a large mixing bowl, combine cheeses, red pepper, mayonnaise, sour cream, mustard, hot sauce, black pepper, herbes de Provence and garlic and onion powders; stir until well incorporated. Serve or store in an airtight container for up to a week.

Restaurant Recipe

# King Street Café

**207 South King Street**
**Morganton, NC 28655**
**828-475-6188**
**www.kingstreetcafe.net**
**Find us on Facebook**

King Street Café is known famously as the place to enjoy fine dining in Morganton. A selection of fine offerings mingled with nightly specials will please those with a palate for fresh herbs and spices, fresh-made sauces, and a special flare not easily found in other cafés. Longtime chef and owner Peter Chan uses the freshest produce from local farms to create tasty entrees, like French onion soup, and a bounty of wild game to create seasonal fare, like trout amandine and roasted duck à l'orange. Finish with a selection from the extensive wine list or an imported beer for the perfect fine-dining experience at an affordable price.

**Wednesday – Saturday: 5:00 pm to 9:00 pm**
**Sunday: 11:00 am to 2:00 pm**

## *Watermelon-Cucumber Salad*

**½ red onion, thinly sliced**
**4 cups diced watermelon**
**1 cucumber, seeded and chopped**
**¼ cup thinly sliced mint**
**Chopped cashews for topping**
**¼ cup olive oil**
**½ lemon, juiced**
**Salt to taste**
**Crumbled goat cheese for topping**

In a bowl filled with cold water, soak onion. Meanwhile, pat dry watermelon and cucumber, then add to another bowl; add mint and toss. Drain onion, transfer to a cheesecloth and squeeze out excess water; add to watermelon-cucumber mixture. Add cashews, olive oil, lemon juice and salt; toss. Top with goat cheese. Enjoy.

**Restaurant Recipe**

# root & vine

**139 West Union Street**
**Morganton, NC 28655**
**828-433-1540**
**www.rootandvinerestaurant.com • Find us on Facebook**

Boasting a wood-burning grill and a wood-fired pizza oven, root & vine's scratch-prepared, New American cuisine is highlighted by globally and locally sourced ingredients, hand-cut meats, fresh seafood, Neapolitan-style pizzas, and seasonal produce. Choose from a selection of 42 rotating beer taps, more than 40 bottled and canned beers, more than 70 wines, and signature cocktails from the full-service bar. Cap off dinner with a bourbon bacon brownie or one of many other daily desserts from the in-house pastry chef. root & vine offers a dining experience like no other in the Greater Burke area.

**Lunch:**
**Monday – Saturday: 11:30 am to 2:30 pm**
**Dinner:**
**Monday – Saturday: 5:00 pm to 9:30 pm**

## Country Ham Gravy

1 pound country ham, diced
3 tablespoons rendered bacon fat
1 jalapeño, minced
½ red bell pepper, small-diced
½ green bell pepper, small-diced
¼ red onion, small-diced
1 clove garlic, minced
1 cup all-purpose flour
¾ cup Pepsi cola
1 quart heavy cream
2 teaspoons cracked black pepper
2 tablespoons Tabasco sauce

In a saucepan over medium heat, slowly render ham in bacon fat. Add peppers and onion; sweat until translucent. Add garlic; sweat no more than 20 seconds. Vigorously whisk in flour. Deglaze with cola, then add heavy cream, black pepper and Tabasco. Bring near to boil, then reduce to simmer, cooking an additional 30 minutes.

Restaurant Recipe

## Pimento Cheese

1 (8-ounce) package cream cheese, softened
¾ cup sour cream
¾ cup mayonnaise
2 tablespoons Tabasco sauce
2 tablespoons Worcestershire
½ pound sharp white Cheddar cheese, shredded
½ pound sharp Cheddar cheese, shredded
¼ cup minced pimentos
Salt and pepper to taste

In a food processor or stand mixer, purée or beat cream cheese, sour cream, mayonnaise, Tabasco and Worcestershire until smooth. Fold in cheeses and pimentos. Adjust seasoning to taste with salt and pepper.

Restaurant Recipe

**100 West Union Street**
**Morganton, NC 28655**
**828-475-1082**
**www.treatnc.com • Find us on Facebook**

Located in Downtown Morganton, Treat is a quirky restaurant and gift shop that keeps things fresh by seasonally rotating its decor, gift shop merchandise, cuisine, and homemade refreshments. The staff at Treat believe that treats are different for every individual and wish to help everyone find a treat of their own. After a browse through the gift shop, stop by for a delicious dishes, ranging from refreshing salads and soups to sandwiches, sides, pastas, tacos, and more. Top your meal off with a handmade cocktail, beer, or a glass of exquisite wine. Stop by today for treats you don't want to miss.

**Wednesday – Saturday: 11:00 am to 9:00 pm**

## *Spinach-Mozzarella Quiche*

**½ pound butter**
**3 cups spinach**
**1½ yellow onions, chopped**
**4 teaspoons salt, divided**
**1 teaspoon pepper**
**3 cups flour**
**1 teaspoon sugar**
**2 cups ice water**
**1 dozen eggs**
**1 quart half-and-half**
**¾ cups grated mozzarella cheese**

Cube butter; freeze immediately. In a skillet over medium-high heat, sauté spinach and onion with 2 teaspoons salt and pepper; drain. In a food processor, combine flour, remaining salt, sugar and frozen butter; pulse until dough reaches a wet-sand texture, slowly adding 1 tablespoon ice water at a time as needed, and forms a ball around the blade. Do not overmix or add too much water. Refrigerate 30 minutes; roll out on a floured surface, then transfer to a nonstick-sprayed springform pan, trimming excess. Beat together eggs and half-and-half; fold in mozzarella then spinach mixture. Pour mixture into pan. Bake on a half-sheet pan at 350° for 1 hour or until quiche has risen and is light brown. If browning too quickly, cover with foil and bake at lower temperature until set.

**Restaurant Recipe**

## *Aunt Magnolia's Yum Yum Coffee Cake*

**1 cup sugar**
**2 eggs**
**1 stick butter, softened**
**1 teaspoon vanilla extract**
**2 cups flour**
**1 teaspoon baking soda**
**1 teaspoon baking powder**
**½ teaspoon salt**
**1 cup buttermilk**

Preheat oven to 350°. In a bowl, beat together sugar, eggs, butter and vanilla. In another bowl, combine flour, baking soda, baking powder and salt. Alternately add dry mixture and buttermilk into wet mixture, stirring after each addition. Transfer to a buttered 9x13-inch baking dish.

### *Topping:*

**1 cup chopped nuts**
**1 cup sugar**
**⅓ cup packed brown sugar**
**1 teaspoon cinnamon**
**½ cup melted butter**

In a bowl, stir together ingredients until combined. Mixture will be lumpy. Add to top of batter, then bake 25 to 30 minutes.

**Family Favorite**

# Red Brick Deli

**89 Tennessee Street**
**Murphy, NC 28906**
**828-837-9090**
**Find us on Facebook**

Opened in May 2015, Red Brick Deli serves up tasty meals and sweet treats in Downtown Murphy. Sample a variety of deli sandwiches, like corned beef, pastrami, Reuben, and more. If you're feeling adventurous, order your sandwich overstuffed. You might also try a wrap, like the Cuban, the Italian, or one with turkey and Virginia ham, or a Sabrett hot dog in natural casing. Red Brick Deli also serve house-made deli salads using egg, tuna, or chicken, but you can also order an antipasto salad or chef's salad. Finish up with a slice of authentic key lime pie with graham cracker crust, brownies, or ice cream.

**Tuesday – Saturday: 11:00 am to 3:00 pm**

## *Egg Salad*

**3 dozen eggs, large-chopped**
**1 cup mayonnaise**
**¼ cup sweet relish**
**1 tablespoon mustard**
**Salt and pepper to taste**

In a bowl, combine all ingredients, mixing until combined. If mixture seems dry, adjust to desired consistency with more mayonnaise. Enjoy!

**Restaurant Recipe**

## *Seasonal Pumpkin Pie*

### *Crust:*

**10 cups graham cracker crumbs**
**1 cup sugar**
**3¾ cups melted butter**

In a large bowl, blend graham cracker crumbs, sugar and butter. Divide between 5 (10-inch) springform pans; freeze.

### *Filling:*

**13 eggs**
**6¾ pounds pure pumpkin**
**5 cups sugar**
**1⅓ cups packed brown sugar**
**1½ tablespoons salt**
**2 tablespoons plus 2 teaspoons ground cinnamon**
**1 tablespoon plus 1 teaspoon ground ginger**
**1½ teaspoons ground cloves**
**4 cups plus 1½ cups milk**
**4½ cups evaporated milk**

Preheat oven to 425°. In a stand mixer, combine eggs and pumpkin, beating until mixed. In a bowl, mix together sugars, salt and spices; add to stand mixer bowl on low speed. Slowly pour in milk, then evaporated milk, beating until combined. Pour into frozen crusts and bake 58 minutes or until set. Refrigerate before serving. Enjoy.

**Restaurant Recipe**

# Lynn's Place

**237 East Main Street**
**Robbinsville, NC 28771**
**828-479-9777**
**Find us on Facebook**

Lynn's Place is a family-owned eatery that has been serving the Robbinsville community more than 14 years. Guests may visit for lunch or dinner, and the restaurant even offers catering. Stop in and enjoy a fresh salad bar; appetizers, like hot wings and loaded French fries; hand-cut steaks; fresh hamburgers, like Charlie's mushroom burger and the bacon burger; a variety of homemade sides, from corn nuggets to fried okra; and homemade desserts, like apple cobbler and coconut cream pie. Everything is made to order. Stop by to dine on Southern comfort food at its finest.

**Monday – Saturday: 11:00 am to 9:00 pm**
**Sunday: 11:00 am to 2:30 pm**

## *Potato Salad*

**12 to 14 russet potatoes, large-diced**
**Salt and pepper to taste**
**½ red onion, chopped**
**2 ½ tablespoon relish**
**3 boiled eggs, chopped**
**1 teaspoon mustard**
**Mayonnaise to taste**

Add potatoes to a large stockpot and cover with water; bring to a boil, then cook 15 minutes or until tender but still firm. Drain water and season potatoes with salt and pepper. Add onion, relish, eggs and mustard; stir to combine. Add mayonnaise a little at a time, stirring after each addition, until desired consistency is reached. Refrigerate in a sealable container if not serving immediately.

**Restaurant Recipe**

# Scoggin's Seafood & Steakhouse

**300 Chimney Rock Road**
**Rutherfordton, NC 28139**
**828-287-3167**
**www.scogginsseafoodandsteakhouse.com**

Scoggin's Seafood & Steakhouse has been serving the Rutherford County area since 1959. Guests will enjoy tasty appetizers, like shrimp cocktails and oysters on the half shell; salads; fresh-made seafood, like deviled crabs and scallops; hand-cut steaks; barbecue plates; chicken dinners; sandwiches; and more. On nice days, the restaurant also offers outdoor dining, so guests can warm up on the patio while enjoying a delicious meal. Come see why Scoggin's Seafood & Steakhouse has been around for sixty years.

**Tuesday – Saturday: 4:00 pm until**

## *Watergate Salad*

**1 (3.4-ounce) box pistachio pudding mix**
**8 ounces Cool Whip**
**2 cups crushed pineapple**
**8 ounces mini marshmallows**

Strain pineapple to remove excess liquid. In a bowl, mix all ingredients until well combined. Enjoy.

Restaurant Recipe

## *Orange Salad*

**½ cup mandarin orange slices**
**2 cups crushed pineapple**
**⅓ cup prepared orange Jell-O**
**8 ounces Cool Whip**
**½ cup cottage cheese**

Strain oranges and pineapple to remove excess liquid. In a bowl, mix all ingredients until combined. Enjoy.

Restaurant Recipe

**4004 NC-105, Suite 8**
**Sugar Mountain, NC 28604**
**828-268-9600**
**www.reidscafeandcatering.com • Find us on Facebook, Instagram, & Tumblr**

Reid's Café is a labor of love by Tina Houston, owner of Reid's Catering Co., established in 1999. Reid's Café uses the highest quality ingredients available to prepare made-to-order soups, handcrafted sandwiches, scratch-made pastries, elegant salads, house-made dressings, and so much more. Eschewing industrially grown or processed foods, Reid's sources fresh seafood and farm goods from local and regional purveyors to ensure only the freshest taste for each guest. The café also offers natural wines, handmade cocktails, and beer to complement the chefs' choice of cured meat and cheeses. Stop by Reid's Café & Catering Co. for soothing atmosphere, scrumptious eats, and friendly staff.

**Monday – Saturday: 11:00 am to 9:30 pm**

## *Sunburst Trout with Creamed Corn & Charred Salsa*

*Charred Salsa:*

**1 cup small sweet peppers**
**1 cup cherry tomatoes**
**1 green onion, thinly sliced**
**1 teaspoon extra virgin olive oil**
**1 teaspoon apple cider vinegar**
**Salt and pepper to taste**

Char peppers and tomatoes over open fire or blister in a sauté pan. Cut peppers into ¼-inch rings and tomatoes in half; add to a bowl. Add green onion, oil, vinegar, salt and pepper. Mix until combined.

*Creamed Corn:*

**3 ears corn**
**1 small pinch each cumin, fennel seed, cayenne and celery seed**
**1 teaspoon butter**
**3 cloves garlic, minced**
**1 tablespoon dry sherry**
**1 cup heavy cream**
**¼ cup freshly chopped basil**
**Salt and pepper to taste**

Shuck and cut corn from cobs into a bowl; run back of knife over cobs to remove corn "milk." Discard cobs and set bowl aside. Toast dry spices in a medium saucepan over medium heat; once aromatic, add butter and garlic, stirring until butter browns. Deglaze with sherry; add cream and corn, stirring frequently until corn is tender. Add basil, salt and pepper.

*Sunburst Trout:*

**2 tablespoons vegetable oil**
**2 filets Sunburst or other North Carolina trout, rinsed, dried and chilled**
**Salt and pepper to taste**

Add oil to medium sauté pan; heat on high until oil begins to smoke. Season trout skin with salt and pepper. Carefully place trout in pan, skin side down, and cook 4 minutes. Flip trout; rest 1 minute. Add Charred Salsa and Creamed Corn to a bowl, side by side. Top with filets. Serves 2.

**Restaurant Recipe**

# LAVENDER B·I·S·T·R·O

**82 North Trade Street**
**Tryon, NC 28782**
**828-440-1140**
**www.lavenderbistronc.com • Find us on Facebook**

Welcome to Lavender Bistro, a charming French–New American restaurant located in the beautiful rolling foothills of the Appalachian Mountains in western North Carolina. Lavender Bistro offers a wide variety of delicious food and beverage options to make sure that you feel right at home each time you visit. Whether it's fresh seafood, fine wines, the famous Lavender BLT, or a scrumptious salad you're looking for, you'll leave satisfied every time. Lavender Bistro also offers catering excellent for any special occasion, from luncheons to rehearsal dinners. Visit Lavender Bistro for French–New American cuisine with a unique flair.

Lunch:
**Monday – Saturday: 11:30 am to 3:00 pm**
Dinner:
**Monday – Saturday: 5:30 pm to 9:00 pm**
Sunday Brunch:
**11:30 am to 3:00 pm**

## *Chocolate-Dipped Coconut Macaroons*

**¾ cup sweetened condensed milk**
**¼ teaspoon almond extract**
**1½ teaspoons vanilla extract**
**¼ teaspoon fine salt**
**1 large egg white**
**3 cups shredded unsweetened coconut, divided**
**1 (4-ounce) bar semisweet chocolate, chopped**

Preheat oven to 350°. In a bowl, combine condensed milk, extracts, salt and egg white; whisk until thoroughly combined. Stir in 2⅓ cups coconut, mixing with a spatula until sticky and moldable. Form into balls with a sorbet scoop, then roll in remaining coconut. Arrange on a silicone-lined baking sheet; bake 20 minutes and cool 20 minutes. Meanwhile, place three-quarters of chocolate in a double boiler over simmering water; stir frequently, scraping down sides to avoid scorching, until chocolate is melted. Remove from heat; stir in remaining chocolate. Dip base of macaroons about ⅛ inch into chocolate. Place macaroons chocolate side down on parchment paper to harden.

**Family Favorite**

## *French Onion Soup*

**¼ cup butter**
**1 teaspoon sugar**
**3 onions, thinly sliced**
**1 tablespoon all-purpose flour**
**½ cup red wine**
**2 (10.5-ounce) cans condensed beef broth**
**1 French baguette**
**8 ounces Swiss cheese, sliced**

In a 4-quart saucepan, melt butter; stir in sugar. Add onions and sauté 10 minutes or until golden brown; stir flour into onions until well blended. Add 2½ cups water, wine and beef broth. Bring to a boil, reduce heat to low and cover; simmer 10 minutes. Cut 4 1-inch-thick slices of French bread, reserving remaining bread to serve with soup; toast bread slices in oven at 325° about 10 minutes or until browned. Ladle soup into 4 (12-ounce) oven-safe bowls. Place 1 slice toasted bread on top of soup in each bowl. Fold Swiss cheese to fit on top of bread in each bowl. Place bowls on a cookie sheet and bake at 425° for 10 minutes or until cheese is melted. Serve with reserved French bread.

**Family Favorite**

**9930 Highway 16**
**West Jefferson, NC 28694**
**336-982-3060**
**www.mountainaireseafood.com • Find us on Facebook**

Tucked away in the heart of Ashe County, just off the Blue Ridge Parkway, Mountain Aire Seafood & Steaks awaits your visit. Featuring an extensive menu, Mountain Aire offers some of the best seafood and steaks in the region. After a day spent canoeing or fishing for smallmouth bass, dine in comfort on a selection of dishes. Try tasty appetizers, like shrimp cocktails and fried mushrooms; delicious entrees, like fried catfish and hand-cut steaks; and sweet desserts, like funnel cake sticks and apple fritters. Come see why the *Ashe Mountain Times* chose Mountain Aire Seafood & Steak as the best of the best seafood restaurant in Ashe County.

**Call for Hours**

## *Homemade Potato Soup*

**2 pounds russet potatoes**
**1 stick butter, divided**
**2 yellow onions, diced**
**Dash salt plus more to taste**
**¼ cup flour**
**3 cups milk**
**2 eggs, boiled, peeled and chopped**
**Salt and pepper to taste**

Wash and cut potatoes into chunks; add to a stockpot with water to cover and boil until fork-tender. Meanwhile, heat 1 tablespoon butter in a skillet; add onions and dash salt, then sauté until golden. Drain potatoes; add remaining butter, stirring until melted. Add flour to make a paste, then stir to coat potatoes. Add milk and stir in eggs; simmer until thickened. Season with salt and pepper to taste.

**Restaurant Recipe**

# Piedmont

JACKSON

# Five POINTS PUBLIC HOUSE

est 2017

**304 East Main Street**
**Albemarle, NC 28001**
**704-550-9647**
**www.5pointspublichouse.com • Find us on Facebook**

Established in the heart of Downtown Albemarle in October 2017, Five Points Public House offers an upscale pub atmosphere that features a classic American menu of favorites. The restaurant offers the finest and freshest ingredients available, all used in delicious dishes that are made to order by a talented culinary team. In addition to offering a comfortable atmosphere and tasty food, Five Points Public House is passionate about its bar selections, including a rotating selection of craft, draft, and local beer.

**Monday – Thursday: 11:30 am to 10:00 pm**
**Friday & Saturday: 11:30 am to midnight**
**Sunday: 11:00 am to 9:00 pm**

## *Pimento Cheese Dip*

**4 cups shredded mild Cheddar cheese**
**19.2 ounces cream cheese, softened**
**¼ cup mayonnaise**
**3.6 ounces jalapeño peppers, sliced**
**9.6 ounces pimentos, diced**
**2 teaspoons garlic powder**
**1 teaspoon onion powder**
**1 teaspoon cayenne pepper**
**3 teaspoons kosher salt**
**2 teaspoons ground pepper**

In a large mixing bowl, combine all ingredients, stirring until a creamy texture is achieved. Serve warm or cold. Pimento Cheese Dip can be refrigerated in an airtight bowl for up to 7 days.

**Restaurant Recipe**

# Off the Square

**114 South 2nd Street**
**Albemarle, NC 28001**
**704-986-0621**
**www.offthesquarenc.com • Find us on Facebook**

Off the Square is a casual, upscale restaurant focused on creating an unforgettable dining experience by using local ingredients to craft gourmet cuisine from scratch. The restaurant offers attentive service, local and imported wines, and a large selection of craft beers. Guests can also enjoy a range of menu items, like steaks, salmon, pasta, burgers, sandwich specials, crab cakes, soups, salads, and a great assortment of desserts. Check out the revolving daily specials and delicious monthly dinner features. Welcome and enjoy!

**Monday – Thursday: 11:00 am to 9:00 pm**
**Friday: 11:00 am to 10:00 pm**
**Saturday: 10:30 am to 10:00 pm**

## *Herb-Roasted Chicken*

**½ cup chicken stock**
**1 tablespoon garlic butter**
**¾ teaspoon each dried parsley, sage, rosemary and thyme**
**¼ cup plus ⅓ cup white wine, divided**
**2 cups heavy cream**
**Salt and pepper to taste**
**4 (5-ounce) chicken breasts**
**2 teaspoons chopped fresh thyme**
**2 teaspoons chopped fresh parsley**
**1 tablespoon olive oil**

Preheat oven to 375°. In a large saucepan over medium heat, combine stock, garlic butter, dried herbs and ¼ cup wine; reduce by half. Stir in heavy cream and salt and pepper to taste; reduce until thickened. Rub chicken with fresh thyme, fresh parsley, salt and pepper; arrange in a large roasting pan. Drizzle with oil and pour remaining wine into bottom of pan. Bake 30 minutes or until cooked through. Broil on high 3 minutes or until skin browns. Remove from oven, slice on a bias, fan out on a plate and spoon prepared sauce over top. Garnish with fresh parsley.

**Restaurant Recipe**

## *The Infamous Quiche*

**1 (9-inch) premade pie crust**
**12 eggs**
**2 tablespoons garlic butter**
**Salt and pepper to taste**
**½ cup grated Cheddar cheese**
**½ cup grated provolone cheese**
**½ cup grated Parmesan cheese**
**Assorted fillings of choice to taste (spinach, vegetables, crispy bacon, chorizo, etc.)**

Preheat oven to 350°. Bake pie crust 10 to 15 minutes until lightly browned; set aside. In a large mixing bowl, combine eggs, butter, salt and pepper; whisk until incorporated. Fold in cheeses and desired fillings. Pour egg mixture into crust and bake 1 hour and 15 minutes.

**Restaurant Recipe**

**2432 Tribek Court**
**Burlington, NC 27215**
**336-437-8373**
**www.delancysrestaurant.com**
**Find us on Facebook**

Opened in 1999, Delancy's Restaurant is a family-owned business serving up some of the best home-cooked meals in Burlington. Specializing in comfort food, Delancy's offers dishes made from scratch using fresh, quality ingredients, which sets the restaurant apart from its competitors. Popular menu items are the meatloaf and chicken pie with pinto beans. Guests also love the scratch-made mashed potatoes, pimento cheese sandwiches, hand-cut fries, and the delicious hot chips. Besides dining in, Delancy's also offers catering and even boasts a private space capable of seating up to 24 guests. Give Delancy's a try, and they'll have you believing that your grandmother is in the kitchen doing all the cooking.

**Monday – Saturday: 11:00 am to 9:00 pm**

## *Chocolate Chess Pie*

**3 cups sugar**
**¾ cup cocoa**
**4 tablespoons cornstarch**
**6 egg yolks**
**½ cup melted butter**
**2¼ cups evaporated milk**
**1 teaspoon vanilla extract**
**2 (9-inch) deep-dish pie shells**

Preheat oven to 350°. In a bowl, combine sugar, cocoa and cornstarch; mix well. Add yolks and butter; mix well. Slow stir in evaporated milk. Stir in vanilla. Divide filling evenly between pie shells. Bake 30 to 40 minutes or until firm.

**Restaurant Recipe**

## *Japanese Fruit Pie*

**1 cup sugar**
**½ cup melted butter**
**2 eggs**
**1 teaspoon apple cider vinegar**
**1 teaspoon vanilla extract**
**½ cup shredded coconut**
**½ cup chopped pecans**
**½ cup raisins**
**1 (9-inch) deep-dish pie shell**

Preheat to 350°. In a stand mixer, cream together sugar and butter. Beat in eggs. Stir in remaining ingredients until well combined. Pour into a pie shell. Bake 40 to 45 minutes or until firm.

**Family Favorite**

Harrison's

# Harrison's Restaurant

**2773 South Church Street**
**Burlington, NC 27215**
**336-584-0444**
**www.harrisonsburlington.com • Find us on Facebook**

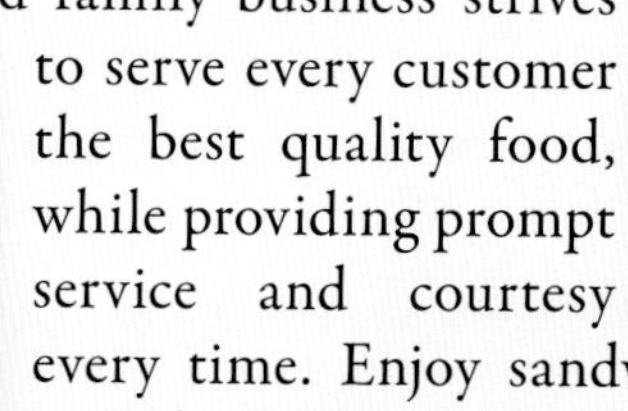

Harrison's Restaurant has been in operation since 1979. A featured restaurant at New Market Square since 1986, this locally owned family business strives to serve every customer the best quality food, while providing prompt service and courtesy every time. Enjoy sandwiches, shish kebab platters, teriyaki chicken, and so much more. Relax in a casual, family-friendly atmosphere and observe wall-mounted artwork created by local artists while you enjoy your meal. Harrison's has had the pleasure of serving generations of families. Come be next in line for a delicious meal with friendly service.

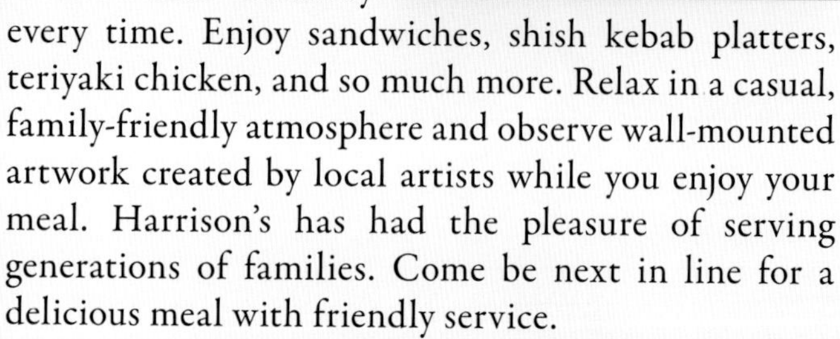

**Daily: 11:00 am to 9:00 pm**

## *Marinated Tenderloin Skewers*

**½ cup salt**
**½ cup ground black pepper**
**⅓ cup granulated onion**
**⅓ cup granulated garlic**
**¼ cup dried oregano**
**1 cup paprika**
**1 pork tenderloin (any size), cut into bite-size pieces**
**4 cups vegetable oil**
**3 cups lemon juice**
**Cut vegetables of choice (peppers, onions, etc.), optional**

To a zip-close plastic bag, add all dry ingredients; shake. Add meat to bag, then oil and lemon juice. Toss with hands to distribute seasoning; marinate in refrigerator at least 6 hours but up to 12 for best results. Remove meat from bag and slide on to skewers, alternating with cut up bell peppers, onions, etc., if desired. Preheat grill to medium (or medium-high if you enjoy a char on your meat) and cook until a meat thermometer inserted into tenderloin reads 145°. A pink tint in the center of meat is normal, so do not overcook meat by attempting to brown it all the way through. Marinated Tenderloin Skewers pair perfectly with baked beans, potato salad, slaw or tossed salad. Happy grilling!

**Restaurant Recipe**

# TickleMyRibs

## REAL CAROLINA BBQ

**1183 University Drive, Suite 101**
**Burlington, NC 27215**
**336-538-0227**
**www.tmrbbq.com • Find us on Facebook**

Tickle My Ribs is a family-owned and -operated restaurant that focuses on providing great food at an affordable price. By using recipes that have been passed down from generation to generation, Tickle My Ribs creates signature flavors that can be enjoyed in their pork, beef brisket, ribs, wings, and chicken. All of the meat is hickory smoked in the restaurant, low 'n' slow, for that tender, juicy, fall-off-the-bone meat that keeps customers coming back for more. All this finger-lickin' food is served up in a modern facility with that traditional Southern-hospitality feel. Pay Tickle My Ribs a visit and discover why it's simply impossible to leave unsatisfied.

**Tuesday – Sunday: 11:00 am to 9:00 pm**

## *Baked Beans*

**6 slices thick-sliced bacon, divided**
**2 (28-ounce) cans baked beans**
**1 cup packed dark brown sugar**
**1½ tablespoons chili powder**
**2 teaspoons ground cumin**
**¼ teaspoon yellow mustard**
**¼ teaspoon Worcestershire sauce**

Preheat oven to 350°. Chop 2 slices bacon into ¼-inch-wide pieces; transfer to a medium saucepan over medium heat, spreading evenly over bottom with a spatula. Cook several minutes to render fat, taking care to prevent bacon crisping. Add baked beans to saucepan, stirring lightly to fold in bacon. Crumble brown sugar into beans; stir until dissolved. Add chili powder and cumin; stir to combine. Stir in mustard and Worcestershire. Simmer beans over medium-low heat until heated through, stirring constantly to prevent sticking or clumping; transfer to a lidded, oven-safe dish. In a skillet over medium heat, lightly brown remaining bacon. Cut bacon slices in half, arrange evenly over top of beans, cover with lid and bake 15 minutes. Remove lid, set broil to high and broil 5 to 10 minutes, checking after 5 minutes for desired firmness of bacon and caramelization of beans. Be careful not to burn. Remove from oven and let sit 5 minutes before serving.

**Restaurant Recipe**

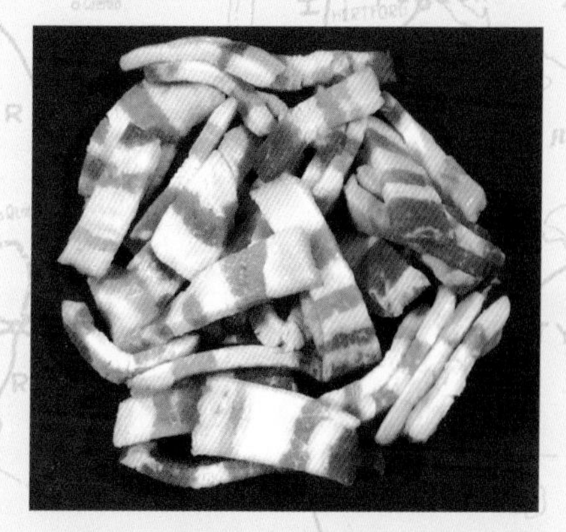

# Crook's Corner

**610 West Franklin Street**
**Chapel Hill, NC 27516**
**919-929-7643**
**www.crookscorner.com • Find us on Facebook**

Crook's Corner has been described as "sacred ground for Southern foodies," offering a "sumptuous take on Southern comfort food." When you arrive, expect delicious food in a casual setting: a cozy dining room wrapped with rotating local art. The menu features seasonal specials, like fried oysters, and classics, like grilled steaks with long-simmering bordelaise. Sides abound, with everything from collards to black pepper cornbread. The restaurant also serves homemade desserts, like banana pudding and Mount Airy chocolate soufflé cake. A selection of tasty wines, North Carolina craft beers, precise top-notch standards, and craft cocktails complement your meal perfectly. Stop by this American classic for quality food and timeless appeal.

Dinner:
**Tuesday – Thursday: 5:30 pm to 9:00 pm**
**Friday & Saturday: 5:30 pm to 9:30 pm**
**Sunday: 5:30 pm to 9:00 pm**
Brunch:
**Sunday: 10:30 am to 2:00 pm**

## *Atlantic Beach Pie*

*Recipe by Chef Bill Smith*

### *Crust:*

**3 sleeves saltine crackers**
**6 tablespoons sugar**
**2 sticks unsalted butter, softened**

In a bowl, crush crackers into a coarse meal. Mix in sugar. Knead in butter until it holds together in a crumbly-doughy consistency. Divide dough in half and press each into 2 (9-inch) pies pans; chill. When set, bake at 350° for 17 minutes or until slightly browned.

### *Filling:*

**8 egg yolks**
**2 (14-ounce) cans sweetened condensed milk**
**½ cup lemon juice**
**½ cup lime juice**

Meanwhile, beat all filling ingredients together in a bowl until well combined. Remove crusts from oven and divide filling between them. Return to oven, baking 15 minutes or until set at centers. Chill pies before cutting. Atlantic Beach Pie pairs great with fresh whipped cream and coarse sea salt.

**Restaurant Recipe**

## *Shrimp & Grits*

*The late Bill Neal, the original chef of Crook's Corner, is popularly credited with elevating shrimp and grits to the dish we know today.*

**4 cups water**
**1 cup grits (not instant)**
**½ teaspoon salt**
**4 tablespoons butter**
**1 cup grated Cheddar cheese**
**½ cup grated Parmesan cheese**
**Tabasco sauce or cayenne pepper to taste**
**6 slices bacon, diced and cook crisp with grease reserved**
**1 pound fresh shrimp, peeled**
**1 cup flour, seasoned with salt and pepper**
**2 cups sliced mushrooms**
**½ cup sliced scallions**
**1 clove garlic, minced**
**1 lemon, juiced**

In a large pot, bring 4 cups water to a boil; stir in grits and salt. Reduce heat to simmer and cook about 20 minutes or until thickened. Stir in butter and cheeses until melted and combined. Add Tabasco to taste, then keep warm. In a skillet over high heat, add bacon grease. Dust shrimp with flour and sauté, stirring constantly, in skillet, taking care not to crowd them. When they begin to color, add mushrooms, continuing to cook 4 minutes or until nearly done. Add garlic and toss once; add lemon juice, scallions and Tabasco to taste. Serve over top of grits. Garnish with cooked bacon.

**Restaurant Recipe**

## Sutton's Drug Store

**159 East Franklin Street**
**Chapel Hill, NC 27514**
**919-942-5161**
**www.suttonsdrugstore.com • Find us on Facebook**

Since 1923, in addition to being a neighborhood pharmacy, Sutton's Drug Store has been serving the Chapel Hill community an impressive selection of hometown specialties, old-fashioned flavored sodas, and hand-spun milkshakes. With a small counter and a few booths, Sutton's serves up a variety of great food, including handcrafted burgers, hot dogs, sandwiches, salads, and wraps. The pharmacy-diner combo also carries a wide selection of old-fashioned and modern candies that make the perfect sweet gift, holiday treat, or quick taste of something new to satisfy your sweet tooth. Stop in for coffee at this unique Chapel Hill landmark and stay for the charm.

**Monday – Friday: 7:00 am to 6:30 pm**
**Saturday: 7:00 am to 4:30 pm**
**Sunday: 9:00 am to 3:00 pm**

## Reese's Chocolate-Banana Shake

**½ cup milk**
**4 generous scoops chocolate ice cream**
**1 ripe banana**
**¼ cup chopped Reese's peanut butter cups**
**Whipped cream for topping, optional**

To a blender, add milk and ice cream. Slice banana and add to blender. Blend until smooth. When smooth, add peanut butter cups and blend again. If peanut butter cups are added early, the coldness of the ice cream will harden them, preventing them from mixing well. Once incorporated, pour into a glass and top with whipped cream before serving, if desired.

**Restaurant Recipe**

## Old-Fashioned Egg Cream

**4 tablespoons chocolate syrup**
**1 cup carbonated water**
**1 cup milk**

In a 20-ounce glass, pour all ingredients; stir thoroughly until combined. Make sure to leave enough room for foam. Mixing in a blender will cause carbonated water to become flat so stirring by hand is preferred. Enjoy.

**Restaurant Recipe**

LIVE MUSIC

# The Local

**105 East 5th Street**
**Charlotte, NC 28202**
**704-347-0035**
**www.thelocalcharlotte.com**
**Find us on Facebook**

Welcome to The Local, a restaurant and bar with a low-key atmosphere, where you will feel right at home. The restaurant is conveniently located in the heart of Uptown Charlotte, just steps away from Spectrum Center, Discovery Place, BB&T Ballpark, and other exciting attractions. The Local connects Queen City residents and visitors with what they crave—flavorful meals, classic drinks, and outstanding happy hour specials. Gather up your friends for lunch, dinner, or late-night fun, and the friendly and attentive staff will be ready to serve you. Your next Uptown Charlotte stop is right around the corner.

**Daily: 11:00 am to 2:00 am**

HAPPY HOUR

## *Blackened Chicken Bacon Alfredo*

**1 cup heavy cream**
**2 cups shredded mild Cheddar cheese**
**6 ounces cavatappi pasta, cooked and drained**
**Salt and pepper to taste**
**4 ounces cooked, shredded chicken breast**
**1 tablespoon blackened seasoning**
**¼ cup grated Parmesan cheese**
**3 strips bacon, cooked and finely chopped**

In a skillet over medium heat, add heavy cream. Slowly stir in cheese, ensuring cheese is melted after each addition. Stir in pasta, salt and pepper. In another skillet over medium-high heat, sear chicken in blackened seasoning, stirring until coated; using a meat thermometer, ensure chicken heats to at least 165°. Transfer cheese-pasta mixture to a dinner bowl; top with chicken. Garnish with Parmesan and bacon. Enjoy.

**Restaurant Recipe**

## *Sriracha Impossible Burger*

**1 tablespoon olive oil**
**1 (3-ounce) vegan Impossible patty**
**1 gourmet pretzel bun**
**1 leaf romaine lettuce**
**2 slices tomato**
**1 thick-cut slice red onion**
**1 jalapeño, sliced into coins**
**1 teaspoon vegan sriracha mayonnaise**

In a cast-iron skillet, heat olive oil to 350°. Fry patty in oil until outside is crispy and center is warmed through, flipping once. Toast pretzel bun on grill or in oven; cool. Dress bottom bun with romaine, tomato and onion. Place patty and top with jalapeño. Spread mayonnaise evenly on top bun; top burger and serve.

**Restaurant Recipe**

# Mert's Heart & Soul

**214 North College Street**
**Charlotte, NC 28202**
**704-342-4222**
**www.mertscharlotte.com • Find us on Facebook**

heart Mert's and Soul
Est. 1998

Mert's Heart & Soul is owned and operated by Athens native James Bazzelle and his wife, Reneé. After discovering his culinary talents in high school, James decided to pursue food service as a career. He earned his associate degree in food service management, working in various food service positions before meeting Reneé in Carrollton. They relocated to Charlotte in the 90s, later opening Mert's in 1998. Since its establishment, Mert's has emerged as one of Charlotte's most acclaimed restaurants. Serving Lowcountry- and Gullah-inspired dishes, like shrimp and grits and Charleston red rice, Mert's distinguishes itself from traditional soul food restaurants. Visit Mert's for food from the heart and soul.

**Monday – Thursday: 11:00 am to 9:30 pm**
**Friday: 11:00 am to 11:30 pm**
**Saturday: 9:00 am to 11:30 pm**
**Sunday: 9:00 am to 9:30 pm**

## Salmon Cakes

**1 pound flaked poached salmon**
**¼ cup cracker meal**
**1 small green bell pepper, chopped**
**1 small onion, chopped**
**1 egg, beaten**
**2 tablespoons granulated garlic**
**2 teaspoons adobo**
**Lemon juice to taste**
**Salt to taste, optional**
**2 tablespoons Texas Pete hot sauce**
**Vegetable oil for frying**

In a bowl, mix all ingredients except vegetable oil until combined; shape into 6 patties. Heat 2 tablespoons oil in a nonstick skillet; fry cakes 3 to 5 minutes per side or until golden brown, flipping once. Pairs perfectly with tartar sauce, remoulade or simply a squeeze of lemon.

**Restaurant Recipe**

## Soul Rolls

**1 cup chopped cooked collard greens**
**½ cup cooked black-eyed peas**
**½ cup cooked rice**
**¼ cup chopped cooked chicken**
**10 egg roll wrappers**
**1 egg white, beaten**

Preheat a deep fryer to 350°. In a bowl, mix together collard greens, peas, rice and chicken to make filling. To assemble egg rolls, lay out a wrapper with a corner pointing toward you. Spoon about 3 tablespoons filling onto the bottom third of wrapper; brush beaten egg on top edges. Fold corner pointing toward you over filling, rolling firmly to the halfway point. Fold in left and right corners snugly, continuing to roll until the egg-white-brushed edges seal wrapper to itself. Repeat with remaining wrappers and filling, covering with plastic wrap to prevent drying out. Fry Soul Rolls 5 to 7 minutes or until golden brown; drain on paper towels before enjoying.

**Restaurant Recipe**

**406 East Main Street**
**Clayton, NC 27520**
**919-585-7005**
**www.manningsonmain.com • Find us on Facebook, Instagram & Twitter**

Howard McIntyre Manning grew up immersed in South Carolina's rich culinary traditions, developing a passion for cooking at an early age. He studied culinary arts and hotel & restaurant management at Johnson & Wales' Charleston campus while working in Charleston's restaurant scene. Building on those experiences, Howard and his wife, Jennifer, and their children, Hannah and Henry, realized their dream of opening their own restaurant, Manning's. Manning's pairs Howard's Southern coastal menu with an exciting venue featuring a rooftop patio, a large dining room, an upstairs reception room, and two rooms for private parties. Chef Howard invites you to visit, and as he says, "Whatever you do, do it Manning-style."

**Monday, Wednesday & Thursday: 11:30 am to 9:00 pm**
**Friday: 11:30 am to midnight**
**Saturday: Noon to midnight**
**Sunday: Noon to 9:00 pm**

## *Charleston-Style Grits*

**½ pound butter**
**2 quarts heavy cream**
**3 cups yellow stone-ground grits**
**2 tablespoons salt**
**½ tablespoon white pepper**

In a saucepan, add butter and heavy cream to 2 quarts water; bring to a boil, then stir in grits. Cook grits until thickened and smooth, then season with salt and pepper. Enjoy.

Restaurant Recipe

## *Cole Slaw*

**12 cups mayonnaise**
**4 cups sugar**
**3 cups white vinegar**
**1 teaspoon salt**
**1 teaspoon black pepper**
**4 large heads cabbage, chopped**

In a large mixing bowl, add mayonnaise, vinegar, sugar, salt and pepper; whisk together until smooth. In another bowl, add cabbage; pour mayonnaise mixture over top, then mix well until cabbage is coated and mayonnaise mixture is evenly distributed. Chill before serving. Enjoy.

Restaurant Recipe

# Vinson's
## PUB + EATERY

**800 East Main Street**
**Clayton, NC 27520**
**919-585-7191**
**www.vinsonspub.com • Find us on Facebook**

Vinson's Pub + Eatery is a brand new restaurant in Downtown Clayton. Right on Main Street, Vinson's specializes in good brews, good burgers, and good times. Begin with a starter, like the Bavarian pretzel rolls served with red oak lager cheese dip, and for the main event, bite into a juicy burger, like the black and blue burger served with blue cheese crumbles, lettuce, tomato, and buttermilk ranch mayo on a toasted croissant. With an amazing outdoor seating area and bar made from reclaimed wood from the 100-year-old building, the atmosphere is perfect for your next event or dinner out with the family. Come enjoy a taste of historic Clayton.

**Tuesday – Friday: 11:00 am to 10:00 pm**
**Saturday: 11:00 am to 11:00 pm**
**Sunday: 11:00 am to 8:00 pm**

## *Chicken Salad*

**3 cups mayonnaise**
**1 tablespoon kosher salt**
**1 teaspoon black pepper**
**1 tablespoon celery seed**
**1 tablespoon sugar**
**3 quarts julienned grilled, seasoned chicken breast**
**3 cups halved red grapes**
**1 cup finely diced celery**
**3 cups diced apples**
**1 cup finely diced roasted walnuts**

In a large bowl, mix mayonnaise, salt, pepper, celery seed and sugar until smooth. Gently fold in remaining ingredients until combined. Refrigerate before serving.

**Restaurant Recipe**

## *Fried Catfish Breading*

**8 cups flour**
**2 teaspoons black pepper**
**2 teaspoons granulated garlic**
**2 teaspoons salt**
**3 teaspoons Cajun seasoning**
**2 teaspoons paprika**
**3 teaspoons Chef Paul Prudhomme's Seafood Magic seasoning**

In a bowl, mix all ingredients together until combined. Store in an airtight container or use immediately. To use: lightly coat catfish fillets in breading, then deep fry at 140° until golden brown.

**Restaurant Recipe**

## The Smoke Pit Restaurant

**796 Concord Parkway North**
**Concord, NC 28027**
**704-795-7573**

**1507 West Roosevelt Boulevard**
**Monroe, NC 28110**
**704-289-7427**

**117 East Innes Street**
**Salisbury, NC 28144**
**704-754-8336**
**www.thesmokepitnc.com • Find us on Facebook**

Originally opened in Concord in December 2014, The Smoke Pit Restaurant has since expanded from a small-service eatery to a full-time operation, serving tasty pit-smoked barbecue at three locations to over 700 customers a day. The Smoke Pit chefs really love what they do, and it shows in every dish that leaves the kitchen. From pulled pork and brisket to sides galore, The Smoke Pit has it all. Guests can dine in or order out. The Smoke Pit even offers catering, so you can get the down-home cooking you crave without having to cook it yourself. Visit The Smoke Pit today for great food and great savings.

Concord:
**Monday – Saturday: 11:00 am to 8:00 pm**
Monroe & Salisbury:
**Tuesday – Saturday: 11:00 am to 9:00 pm**
**Sunday: 11:00 am to 6:00 pm**

## *Sweet Potato Casserole*

**3 cups mashed sweet potatoes**
**½ cup packed brown sugar**
**2 large eggs**
**1 teaspoon vanilla extract**
**½ cup milk**
**½ cup melted butter**

Preheat oven to 350° and grease a 9x13-inch casserole dish. In a large bowl, combine potatoes, brown sugar, eggs, vanilla, milk and melted butter; mix thoroughly, then transfer mixture to prepared dish.

### *Topping:*

**½ cup packed brown sugar**
**⅓ cup flour**
**⅓ cup melted butter**
**½ cup chopped pecans**

In a bowl, add all ingredients, mixing until well combined. Evenly sprinkle topping over sweet potato mixture. Bake 30 to 40 minutes or until filling is hot and the top is golden brown. Enjoy.

**Family Favorite**

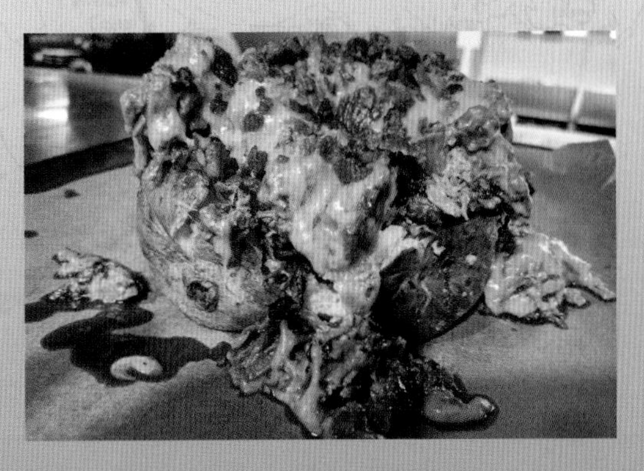

# River Rock Café

**109 Crawford Street**
**Danbury, NC 27016**
**336-593-1015**
**www.riverrockcafe.us • Find us on Facebook**

On the hill between Hanging Rock State Park and the banks of the beautiful Dan River rests River Rock Café, a warm, cozy café serving locals and outdoor enthusiasts. After a day spent hiking, canoeing, or exploring the state park, stop by River Rock for a delicious meal. Sample grilled specialty sandwiches, homemade soups, salads, handmade pizza, flatbreads, brownies, cookies, cobblers, homemade cakes, homemade pies, and premium coffee. Come out to River Rock Café to hike, paddle, and eat.

**Lunch Served Daily**
**Dinner Served Thursday – Saturday**

## *Chicken-Corn Chowder*

**4 chicken bouillon cubes**
**2 pounds boneless, skinless chicken breasts**
**1 tablespoon garlic powder**
**1 tablespoon celery salt**
**1 teaspoon black pepper**
**1 teaspoon Italian seasoning**
**1 small red onion, diced**
**1 small green bell pepper, diced**
**1 (15-ounce) can whole-kernel corn**
**2 cups diced potatoes**
**1 cup flour**
**1 quart half-and-half**
**Crackers or homemade cornbread for serving**

In a large stockpot, add 1 gallon water and bouillon cubes; bring to a boil and add chicken. Boil chicken 30 minutes or until cooked through; remove from pot, shred and set aside. To same pot, add garlic powder, celery salt, black pepper and Italian seasoning; whisk to combine. Stir in onion, bell pepper, corn and potatoes. Add back shredded chicken. Reduce heat to low and simmer 30 minutes. In another bowl, whisk together flour and half-and-half; stir into pot. Simmer 30 minutes more, stirring occasionally. Serve with crackers or homemade cornbread. Makes 2 gallons.

**Restaurant Recipe**

# North Harbor Club

**100 North Harbor Place**
**Davidson, NC 28036**
**704-896-5559**
**www.northharborclub.com • Find us on Facebook**

North Harbor Club offers more than just a meal; it's an experience. Replete with unique decor, guests can enjoy a delicious meal while they take in the intriguing atmosphere, from the large sailboat near the door to the historic watercrafts mounted on the ceilings. Dive in to starters like fried pickles or asparagus fries, and when it's time for the main course, enjoy everything from arugula burgers to coriander-marinated flatiron steaks. When the weather is nice, North Harbor Club offers first-come, first-served waterfront dining on the patio, where guests may also enjoy live music on select nights. Come experience North Harbor Club with your family and friends.

**Sunday – Thursday: 11:00 am to 9:00 pm**
**Friday & Saturday: 11:00 am to 9:30 pm**

## *Carolina Coleslaw*

**2 heads Savoy cabbage, shredded**
**2 cups julienned red cabbage**
**1 cup finely julienned carrots**
**3 cups julienned broccoli stems**
**1½ cups sugar**
**2 cups apple cider vinegar**
**2 cups extra virgin olive oil**
**½ teaspoon cayenne pepper**
**Kosher salt to taste**
**1 teaspoon ground black pepper**

In a bowl, toss together cabbage, carrots and broccoli; set aside. In another bowl, combine remaining ingredients to create a marinade; pour over vegetables and toss. Cover and marinate 1 hour before serving.

**Restaurant Recipe**

## *Basil Hushpuppies*

**3 cups cornmeal**
**1⅓ cups all-purpose flour**
**1 cup sugar**
**½ teaspoon cayenne pepper**
**2 teaspoons baking powder**
**1 teaspoon baking soda**
**1 teaspoon kosher salt**
**2 cups buttermilk**
**1 cup small-diced yellow onion**
**2 tablespoons finely chopped garlic**
**4 eggs, lightly beaten**
**1 cup puréed whole-kernel corn**
**½ cup freshly chopped basil**

Preheat deep fryer to 350°. In a bowl, sift together cornmeal, flour, sugar, cayenne, baking powder, baking soda and salt; make a well in the center. Add remaining ingredients; mix until just damp, taking care not to overmix. Drop tablespoonsful of batter into deep fryer, frying 2 to 2½ minutes or until golden brown. Remove and drain on paper towels.

**Restaurant Recipe**

# BLUE CORN CAFÉ

Latin American Cuisine

716 9th Street
Durham, NC 27705
919-286-9600
www.bluecorncafedurham.com • Find us on Facebook & Instagram

Blue Corn Café opened in June 1997. With a dollar and a dream, owners Antonio Rios and Danielle Martini-Rios set off to serve the public fusion-style flavor of all Latin and South America. They knew staying true to their roots and heritage was important when deciding on what menu items and ingredients to serve. Blue Corn serves everything from Cuban-style beans to authentic hand-rolled empanadas and includes fresh plantains, mangoes, guavas and more in their dishes. Chef Antonio enjoys fusing the flavors of his native country, Mexico, with authentic flavors from the Caribbean and South America. Their mission is to serve simple, organic ingredients prepared on site daily. ¡Provecho!

**Monday – Thursday: 11:30 am to 9:00 pm**
**Friday & Saturday: 11:30 am to 9:30 pm**

## *Cilantro Vinaigrette Dressing*

**1 (15-ounce) can garbanzo beans, rinsed and drained**
**1 bunch fresh cilantro**
**½ teaspoon black pepper**
**½ tablespoon salt**
**½ cup red wine vinegar**
**1 cup olive oil**
**1 cup filtered water**
**1 clove garlic**

In a blender, add garbanzo beans. De-stem cilantro and drop in. Add remaining ingredients and blend on high. Continue blending until desired smoothness reached. Add more olive oil or garbanzo beans to adjust texture as needed. Makes 1 quart.

Restaurant Recipe

# Picnic

**1647 Cole Mill Road**
**Durham, NC 27705**
**919-908-9128**
**www.picnicdurham.com • Find us on Facebook, Instagram & Twitter**

Picnic was opened in February 2016 by Executive Chef Ben Adams, heritage-breed pig farmer Ryan Butler, and self-styled "barbecue man" Wyatt Dickson. This neighborhood barbecue joint features an extensive menu of dishes, from starters and sandwiches to plate lunches and desserts. You'll enjoy fried green tomatoes, chicken wings, pulled pork sandwiches, sliced brisket, blackened catfish, and more. You can even order locally sourced, wood-smoked, hand-pulled whole hog barbecue. Don't leave without sampling a range of delicious sides, from classic mac & cheese to fried okra. Picnic is also available for catering your next big event. The Picnic team hopes to see you soon.

**Sunday – Thursday: 11:00 am to 9:00 pm**
**Friday & Saturday: 11:00 am to 10:00 pm**

## *Baked Beans*

**2 pounds bacon, chopped**
**6 yellow onions, diced**
**6 green bell peppers, diced**
**6 red bell peppers, diced**
**20 cloves garlic, processed in blender**
**2 quarts ketchup**
**2 quarts packed brown sugar**
**3 quarts molasses**
**6 quarts water**
**3 quarts pork stock**
**1½ teaspoons cayenne pepper**
**6 tablespoons black pepper**
**1 cup salt**

In a large stockpot over medium heat, sauté bacon, onion, bell peppers and garlic until tender but not caramelized. Add remaining ingredients; continue cooking until reduced by a fourth.

**Restaurant Recipe**

## *Cornmeal Pound Cake*

**1 pound butter**
**3 cups sugar**
**3 cups all-purpose flour**
**1 cup cornmeal**
**1½ teaspoons baking powder**
**Pinch salt**
**12 eggs**
**1 lemon, zested and juiced**
**1 tablespoon vanilla extract**

Preheat oven to 350°. In a bowl, cream together butter and sugar until fluffy. In another bowl, mix flour, cornmeal, baking powder and salt. In another bowl, beat together eggs, lemon juice, lemon zest and vanilla. Alternately add flour mixture then egg mixture to butter mixture, stirring after each addition. Spray and line with parchment a 4-inch-deep half hotel pan; transfer batter to pan. Bake 45 minutes; lower to 325°, turn cakes and continue baking until golden brown and center bounces back when lightly pressed.

**Restaurant Recipe**

# SOUTHERN ON MAIN

**102 East Main Street**
**Elkin, NC 28621**
**336-258-2144**
**www.southernonmain.com • Find us on Facebook**

The heart of the South has always been its blue-collar workers raised on farms, fields, and ranches. Warm climates and fertile soil have given abundantly to an equally warm people who took those ingredients and created a cuisine and a culture rich in flavor and history. Southern On Main sought to create a menu that celebrates that history and reflects the people who created it: simple, honest, and delightful. Every time they simmer a pot of collard greens, mix a batch of pimento cheese, or bake off a fresh blueberry sonker, it's done in the tradition of sharing wonderful foods with those they love.

**Sunday – Thursday: 11:00 am to 9:00 pm**
**Friday & Saturday: 11:00 am to 10:00 pm**

## *Bread Pudding*

**6 large eggs**
**1½ cups sugar**
**1 cup maple syrup**
**2 cups half-and-half**
**1 tablespoon vanilla extract**
**½ teaspoon salt**
**2 teaspoons ground cinnamon**
**2 loaves white bread, cut into ¾-inch cubes**
**Ice cream and caramel sauce for serving**

In a large bowl, combine eggs, sugar, syrup, half-and-half, vanilla and salt; whisk until smooth. Whisk in cinnamon until incorporated. Lightly grease a 9x13-inch baking dish with nonstick spray; add bread cubes and pour mixture over top. Refrigerate 24 hours to allow bread to soak up liquid. Preheat oven to 350°. Toss bread to redistribute liquid and press together to create an even top. Cover and bake 30 minutes; remove cover and bake 30 more minutes or until pudding is set and beginning to brown. Cool, then serve in bowls with vanilla ice cream and caramel sauce. Enjoy.

**Restaurant Recipe**

## *Pimento Cheese*

**2½ pounds shredded Cheddar cheese**
**1 teaspoon pepper**
**2 teaspoons salt**
**2 cups small-diced roasted red peppers, drained**
**1 cup mayonnaise**
**¼ cup sugar**
**1 tablespoon paprika**
**1 teaspoon hot sauce**
**1 teaspoon Worcestershire sauce**
**1 pound cream cheese, cubed and softened**

In a large bowl, combine all ingredients except cream cheese, working together with hands until incorporated. Add cream cheese and work into mixture with hands, mixing until desired consistency is achieved. Enjoy immediately or refrigerate up to 6 days, sealed in an airtight container.

**Restaurant Recipe**

# Fayetteville Pie Company

**253 Westwood Shopping Center**
**Fayetteville, NC 28314**
**910-483-4097**
**www.fayettevillepiecompany.com**
**Find us on Facebook**

Fayetteville has become an adopted home for Fayetteville Pie Company. This charming pie bakery was inspired to bring a small slice of its family recipes and travels to life, right where it is planted. Owner Leslie Pearson opened the pie shop with her husband, Justin, and knew immediately that the menu would be inspired by the hot, homemade pies her grandmother used to make. In Fayetteville Pie Company's kitchen, a love of entertaining combines with fresh, local ingredients to create delicious, individual, savory and sweet pies that recall a happy childhood spent in your grandmother's kitchen. Come settle down to the taste of home while you reminisce on days gone by.

**Monday – Saturday: 11:00 am to 3:00 pm**

## *Vegetable Makhani*

### *Cucumber Raita:*

**2 cucumbers, washed and cubed**
**1 cup fresh parsley, washed and finely minced**
**4 cups Greek yogurt**
**6 cups mayonnaise**
**¼ cup sugar**
**½ cup white vinegar**
**4 teaspoons lemon juice**

Mix together all ingredients until well combined; set aside.

### *Mango Chutney:*

**3½ cups diced mango**
**½ cup chopped roasted red peppers**
**1½ cups sugar**
**½ cup golden raisins**
**½ cup white vinegar**
**¼ teaspoon ground ginger**
**1 tablespoon lemon juice**
**2 teaspoons curry powder**
**½ teaspoon each ground nutmeg, cinnamon and salt**

Combine mango, peppers, sugar, raisins, vinegar and ginger in saucepan; boil gently, uncovered, 20 minutes or until fruit is tender and mixture is thickened, stirring occasionally. Add lemon juice, curry powder, nutmeg, cinnamon, and salt; continue boiling 5 minutes, then set aside.

*Vegetable Curry:*

**7 cups chopped carrots**
**6 quarts chopped cauliflower**
**4½ cups peeled and diced potatoes**
**6 tablespoons olive oil plus more for coating vegetables**
**1 cup plus 2½ tablespoons kosher salt plus more for coating vegetables**
**1 cup ground cumin plus more for coating vegetables**
**1 cup curry powder**
**5 tablespoons ground turmeric**
**1 cup coriander**
**2 tablespoons cayenne pepper**
**4 tablespoons garlic powder**
**1 tablespoon ground ginger**
**2¼ teaspoons cinnamon**
**2 tablespoons black pepper**
**1 cup sugar**
**6 cups plus 6 tablespoons coconut milk**
**2 cups half-and-half**
**6 tablespoons lemon juice**
**4¾ teaspoons Better Than Bouillon seasoned vegetable base**
**1 cup plus 2 tablespoons minced garlic**
**3 cups tomato paste**
**9 cups diced onion**
**1 (110-ounce) can chickpeas, drained**
**6 cups green peas**
**35 (6-inch) premade deep-dish pie crusts**
**Eggs as needed, beaten for egg wash**

Preheat oven to 425°. Roast vegetables, one at a time, in roasting pan until tender, coating carrots in oil and salt, and cauliflower in oil, salt and cumin; potatoes require no extra seasoning. In a bowl, combine remaining salt with other spices to make spice mix; set aside. In a large bowl, combine liquids and vegetable base with 6 cups water; whisk until blended and set aside. In large pot over medium heat, add oil; add garlic, cooking until fragrant. Add tomato paste and spice mix; heat until smooth paste forms. Add liquids; whisk until brownish-orange, yellow curry sauce forms. Add onion, chickpeas and green peas. Stir in roasted vegetables. Pour into pie crusts, fold crusts galette-style and brush with egg. Bake at 360° for 20 minutes, rotating halfway through. Cool pies; top with Raita and Chutney.

**Restaurant Recipe**
**Executive Chef Martha K. Lee**

## Reverence Farms Café

**6956 South Highway 87**
**Graham, NC 27253**
**336-525-2266**
**www.reverencefarmscafe.com • Find us on Facebook**

Located about two miles from the Village of Saxapahaw, Reverence Farms Café's mission is to show that it's possible to raise and prepare real food from a real farm by serving their own poultry, meats, and eggs as well as produce and dairy from friends and neighbors. At Reverence Farms, animals are treated with reverence and grace, earthworms are cherished, and all critters eat a species-appropriate diet. These practices, in collaboration with local farms and suppliers, ensure you always receive honest food that is seriously local. The café aspires to service as a higher calling and pays a living wage. Everything is simple and scratch-made, so you can taste the love every time.

**Tuesday – Friday: 11:00 am to 8:00 pm**
**Saturday: 10:00 am to 8:00 pm**
**Sunday: 10:00 am to 2:00 pm**

## *Cowboy Cookies*

**2 sticks butter, softened**
**⅔ cup packed brown sugar**
**½ cup white sugar**
**2 eggs**
**1 teaspoon vanilla extract**
**2 cups all-purpose flour**
**2 cups rolled oats**
**1¼ teaspoons baking soda**
**½ teaspoon salt**
**¼ cup flaked coconut**
**½ cup chocolate chips**
**¾ cup raisins**
**¾ cup chopped pecans**

Preheat oven to 350°. In the bowl of a stand mixer, beat together butter and sugars until fluffy; beat in eggs and vanilla. In a separate bowl, whisk together flour, oats, baking soda and salt; add to stand mixer bowl and mix until just combined. Remove bowl from mixer and fold in coconut, chocolate chips, raisins and pecans by hand. Roll into 1-inch balls; arrange on a greased baking sheet, then bake 10 to 14 minutes or until golden brown.

**Restaurant Recipe**

## *Meatloaf*

**1 pound grass-fed ground beef**
**2 pounds mild breakfast sausage**
**4 organic eggs**
**⅓ cup ketchup**
**⅓ cup Dijon mustard**
**1 tablespoon onion powder**
**1 tablespoon Italian seasoning**
**1 small white onion, small-diced**
**Salt and pepper to taste**
**¾ cup breadcrumbs**

Preheat oven to 350°. In a bowl, mix meats until fully incorporated. Add remaining ingredients except breadcrumbs; mix until fully incorporated. Add breadcrumbs; mix until fully incorporated. Transfer mixture to a nonstick-sprayed 5x9-inch loaf pan. Cover with foil and bake 1 hour; remove foil and bake another 15 to 20 minutes to desired color.

**Restaurant Recipe**

# Hatch Sandwich Bar

**268 1st Avenue Northwest**
**Hickory, NC 28601**
**828-322-1196**
**www.hatchsandwich.com • Find us on Facebook**

Hatch Sandwich Bar opened in 2012 with a goal in mind: to serve simple, quick, and tasty food in Downtown Hickory. Co-owners Zach Harkins and Colin Makin wanted a place to create and serve unique sandwiches, salads, and sides in a fun, local environment. The idea for Hatch Sandwich Bar was born. Hatch Sandwich Bar is grateful for the opportunity to serve the Hickory community and for the lifelong friendships that have been made along the way. Stop by today and make some new friends over the special of the day and a beer.

**Monday: 10:30 am to 2:00 pm**
**Tuesday – Friday: 10:30 am to 8:00 pm**
**Saturday: 10:30 am to 3:00 pm**

## *Squash Bisque*

**2 medium onions, chopped**
**2 tablespoons butter**
**4 cups chicken broth**
**4 cups sliced squash**
**¾ cup sliced carrots**
**2 medium potatoes, diced**
**1 teaspoon salt**
**1 teaspoon thyme**
**2 to 4 teaspoons Worcestershire sauce**
**1 pint half-and-half**

In a large saucepan over medium heat, sauté onions in butter. Add broth, squash, carrots, potatoes, salt and thyme; cook until vegetables are tender. Using an immersion blender, puree bisque. Reduce heat to low; add Worcestershire and half-and-half. Heat through and serve.

**Local Favorite**

## *Stuffed Baked Apples*

**4 baking apples**
**⅓ cup dried cranberries**
**⅓ cup slivered almonds**
**½ teaspoon cinnamon**
**½ teaspoon nutmeg**
**2 tablespoons honey**
**½ cup orange juice concentrate**

Preheat oven to 325°. Wash apples and core ¾ of apple, leaving a little in bottom. In a bowl, combine cranberries, almonds, cinnamon and nutmeg; mix well. Stuff each apple with cranberry mixture. Place apples in a 9-inch square baking dish. In another bowl, add honey and orange juice with 2 cups water; mix well. Pour honey mixture over apples. Bake 30 to 40 minutes or until apples are tender.

**Local Favorite**

# Kepley's Barbecue

**1304 North Main Street**
**High Point, NC 27262**
**336-884-1021**
**www.kepleysbarbecue.com • Find us on Facebook**

Since June 1948, Kepley's Barbecue has served High Point with only the best North Carolina–style barbecue, hot dogs, hamburgers, hushpuppies, fries, salads, and cobbler. Kepley's barbecue is prepared using vinegar-based, slow-cooked pork that is hand chopped and served with their signature homemade barbecue slaw. Settle into a plate of pit-cooked barbecue while you take in the charming, country-diner-style atmosphere. Visit Kepley's Barbecue today and experience great food and personal service, where taste meets tradition.

**Monday – Saturday: 8:30 am to 8:30 pm**

## *Hushpuppies*

**2 cups self-rising white cornmeal**
**½ cup self-rising flour**
**1 tablespoon sugar**
**1¼ cups milk**
**1 egg**

Preheat deep fryer to 350°. In a bowl, mix all ingredients until well combined. Drop tablespoon-size dollops of batter into deep fryer. Fry 3 to 4 minutes or until golden brown and floating to surface of oil.

**Customer-Submitted Recipe**

**2600 South Main Street**
**High Point, NC 27263**
**336-885-8101**
**www.peppermillcafe.com • Find us on Facebook**

At The PepperMill Café, you can sink your teeth into delicious down-home cooking. This full-service family-owned restaurant offers a well-rounded menu sure to please diners of all ages. With cuisine steeped in Mediterranean roots, you'll find a range of dishes featuring olive oil and traditional Mediterranean spices, but if that's not your speed, don't worry; the menu offers classics like cheeseburgers and hot dogs for diners who prefer simple dishes to tasty Euro-inspired treats, like gyros and souvlaki. The café also offers catering for customers who need help feeding a crowd at their next big event. Dine at The PepperMill Café for breakfast, lunch, or dinner.

**Monday – Friday: 6:00 am to 9:00 pm**
**Saturday & Sunday: 6:00 am to 2:00 pm**

## *Greek Meatballs*

**5 slices Italian bread, crusts removed**
**1 yellow onion, finely chopped**
**5 cloves garlic, minced**
**1½ teaspoons salt**
**2 pounds ground beef**
**2 eggs**
**One bunch parsley, finely diced**
**One bunch mint, finely diced**
**½ teaspoon pepper**
**2 tablespoons chopped oregano**
**1 lemon, juiced**
**Flour for coating**
**Olive oil for frying**

Brush just enough water over bread to moisten. In a bowl, combine onion, garlic and salt; mash with hands until juices release. Add remaining ingredients except flour and olive oil and work into a rough, dough-like consistency. Roll into 1-inch meatballs, then roll in flour to coat. In a large pan over medium heat, heat a ½-inch-deep layer oil to 350°. Fry meatballs in oil until a nice crust forms, flipping several times.

**Family Favorite**

## *Taco Dip*

**1 yellow onion, large-diced**
**10 cloves garlic, minced**
**2 pounds ground beef**
**Salt and pepper to taste**
**1 tablespoon chili powder**
**1½ tablespoons cumin**
**1 tablespoon dried oregano**
**1 (16-ounce) container sour cream**
**Shredded Mexican four cheese**
**Diced tomatoes**
**Diced green onions**
**Sliced black olives**

In a large skillet over medium-high heat, sauté onions until translucent; add garlic and ground beef. Brown beef; stir in salt and pepper just before completely browned. Reduce heat to low and add chili powder, cumin, oregano and water just shy of covering the meat; simmer, covered, constantly stirring to prevent sticking. When all water is absorbed, layer meat in the bottom of a 9x13-inch dish. Next layer sour cream and cheese. Sprinkle tomato, onion and olives over top. Serve with tortilla chips or on tacos shells and tortillas.

**Family Favorite**

# Crispy's Bar & Grill

3339 Cloverleaf Parkway
Kannapolis, NC 28083
704-956-2831
www.crispysbarandgrill.com
Find us on Facebook

Welcome to a bacon-lover's paradise. At Crispy's Bar & Grill, you will enjoy great service and some of the most delicious, creative bacon dishes in Kannapolis. Just a short drive from Charlotte, Crispy's offers a great beer selection, eclectic atmosphere, world-class service and superb yet unusual food. Dine on dishes like bacon-fried country chicken, honey-sriracha bacon barbecue ribs, bacon-wrapped cheese sticks, bacon burgers, and more. Come out and eat for a great family treat and be prepared to come back again and again.

**Tuesday – Thursday:**
**11:00 am to 9:00 pm**
**Friday & Saturday:**
**11:00 am to 10:00 pm**
**Sunday: 11:00 am to 2:00 pm**

## *Bacon Jam*

**1 pound smoked bacon, chopped**
**1 medium yellow onion, sliced**
**4 cloves garlic, chopped**
**3 tablespoons packed brown sugar**
**Tabasco sauce to taste**
**1 cup brewed coffee**
**¼ cup apple cider vinegar**
**¼ cup maple syrup**
**Pinch black pepper**

In a nonstick skillet, fry bacon in batches until lightly browned and beginning to crisp. Remove bacon from pan, then fry onion and garlic in bacon fat over medium heat until translucent. Transfer bacon, onion and garlic to a heavy-bottom stockpot; stir in remaining ingredients. Simmer 2 hours, stirring every 25 to 30 minutes. Cool 15 to 20 minutes; transfer to food processor and blend to desired consistency.

**Restaurant Recipe**

## *Loaded Bacon Potato Soup*

**6 strips bacon, chopped**
**3 tablespoons butter**
**1 medium yellow onion, chopped**
**3 large cloves garlic, minced**
**⅓ cup all-purpose flour**
**2½ pounds gold potatoes, peeled and diced into ½-inch pieces**
**4 cups chicken stock**
**2 cups milk**
**⅔ cup heavy cream**
**1 ½ teaspoons salt**
**1 teaspoon ground black pepper**
**⅔ cup sour cream**
**Shredded Cheddar cheese, chopped chives, sour cream and cooked bacon for topping, optional**

Place bacon strips in a large Dutch oven over medium heat; cook until crisp and browned. Remove bacon, leaving fat; add butter, then sauté onion 3 to 5 minutes or until tender. Add garlic, cooking about 30 seconds or until fragrant. Whisk in flour until smooth. Add potatoes, chicken stock, milk, cream, salt and pepper; stir well. Bring to a boil; cook 10 minutes or until potatoes are fork-tender. Reduce heat to simmer; remove half soup to a blender and purée until smooth. Return purée to pot. Stir in sour cream and simmer 15 minutes before serving. Top with shredded Cheddar, chives, sour cream and cooked bacon, if desired.

**Restaurant Recipe**

**100 Jerusalem Drive, Suite 106**
**Morrisville, NC 27560**
**919-465-9006**
**www.babymooncafe.com • Find us on Facebook**

Serving authentic Italian cuisine, Babymoon Café is located just minutes away from Raleigh-Durham International Airport. This charming eatery is a favorite lunch and dinner spot of locals. The Babymoon Café team provides comfortable fine dining and catering, from brown-bag lunches to black-tie events. Babymoon Café takes great pride in the Italian culinary tradition and loves sharing it with guests. The extensive menu offers a variety of pizzas, pastas, seafood, steaks, salads, and so much more, providing diners with the chance to try something new every time they visit. Stop by Babymoon Café today for delightful food and beautiful atmosphere.

**Monday – Saturday: 11:00 am to 10:00 pm**

## Veal Saltimbocca

4 tablespoons olive oil, divided
All-purpose flour for coating
3 (2-ounce) cuts veal, pounded
2 pinches each salt and pepper, divided
¼ cup Marsala wine
¼ cup chicken stock
¼ cup premade demi-glace
1 ounce prosciutto, chopped
2 tablespoons sliced, cooked mushrooms
3 ounces fresh mozzarella cheese, grated
¼ cup pitted Kalamata olives
1 tablespoon butter
¾ to 1 cup baby spinach leaves
2 tablespoons minced garlic
4 ounces cooked angel hair pasta

In a skillet, warm 2 tablespoons oil over medium-high heat. Lightly flour veal; add to hot oil. Sear one side; lightly season with 1 pinch each salt and pepper, then sear other side. Remove veal from pan; set aside. Drain oil. Deglaze skillet with wine and stock; add demi-glace, prosciutto, mushrooms, mozzarella, olives and butter. Simmer over medium heat until cheese melts. Return veal to skillet, allowing flour coating to thicken mixture. In another skillet, sauté spinach with garlic and remaining oil, salt and pepper. Serve veal and sauce over pasta with sautéed spinach on the side or over top.

Restaurant Recipe

## Seafood Fra Diavolo

2 tablespoons olive oil
3 ounces calamari, cleaned
10 (51/60-size) shrimp
3 live middleneck clams
6 frozen mussels, thawed
¼ cup minced garlic
Salt and pepper to taste
2 tablespoons crushed red pepper
Dash cayenne pepper
¼ cup white wine
3 large, fresh basil leaves, chiffonaded
½ cup plus 2 tablespoons marinara
4 ounces cooked linguini pasta

In a skillet over medium-high heat, warm oil. Add calamari, shrimp, clams and mussels. Add garlic, salt and peppers; sauté 2 minutes or until seafood is halfway cooked and seasonings have incorporated. Deglaze skillet with wine. Add basil and marinara; simmer over low heat about 2 minutes or until seafood is cooked through. Serve over prepared pasta.

Restaurant Recipe

**541 West Pine Street, Suite 200**
**Mount Airy, NC 27030**
**336-755-2340**
**www.millcreekgeneralstore.com • Order online or on Facebook**

Mill Creek General Store is a family-owned market and deli that specializes in healthy whole-food options, like Amish meats and cheeses, gluten-free flours and foods, non-GMO foods, locally grown and produced goods, fresh-baked breads, and specialty baking and candy supplies. Known as "the whole-foods store of Mount Airy," the deli has become quite the rave. The deli uses only the highest quality Amish meats and cheeses and fresh, local produce to create made-to-order sandwiches, wraps, and salads. Try the Shorty's Mill Italian sandwich, the Chicken Salad Croissant, the Mitchell's Mill Club, or the Dellinger Mill Reuben. Enjoy your order in the dine-in bistro area or take it to go. Let 'em make you a sammich!

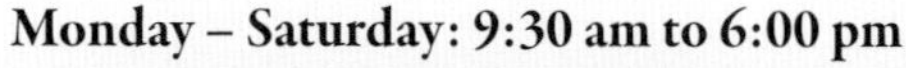

**Monday – Saturday: 9:30 am to 6:00 pm**

## *Peanut Butter Buckeyes*

**2 sticks butter, softened**
**2 cups creamy peanut butter**
**3½ to 4 cups powdered sugar**
**1½ teaspoons vanilla extract**
**3 pounds milk chocolate melting wafers**

In a bowl, thoroughly mix butter, peanut butter, powdered sugar and vanilla; cover with plastic wrap and refrigerate 1 hour. When chilled, roll into 1-inch balls, then arrange in rows on parchment-lined baking sheets; chill in freezer 5 to 7 minutes. Meanwhile, melt chocolate wafers per package directions. Remove balls from freezer; dip into chocolate, using a fork to roll from side to side and leaving a small space uncoated to create the buckeye. Return to baking sheet and refrigerate until set.

**Restaurant Recipe**

## *Cranberry-Pecan Cheeseball*

**½ cup dried cranberries**
**2 cups shredded Cheddar cheese**
**¼ cup maple syrup**
**½ cup chopped pecans plus more for rolling**
**2 (8-ounce) packages cream cheese, softened**
**Chopped fresh parsley for rolling**

In a bowl, mix cranberries, Cheddar, syrup and pecans into cream cheese until well incorporated. Roll into a rough ball, then roll in additional pecans and parsley until coated. Wrap in plastic wrap and shape into a smooth ball. Refrigerate before serving.

**Restaurant Recipe**

# Snappy Lunch

**125 North Main Street**
**Mount Airy, NC 27030**
**336-786-4931**
**www.thesnappylunch.com**

First opened in 1923, Snappy Lunch has stood the test of time. Once a young man working odd jobs in 1943, Charles Dowell later became the sole owner of Snappy Lunch in 1960. In its early days, the restaurant catered to local workers and students (including TV legend Andy Griffith) who enjoyed bologna sandwiches for a nickel and hot dogs for a dime. Dowell continued in that tradition, serving simple sandwiches, hot dogs, and chips until his passing in 2012. During his time at Snappy Lunch, Dowell invented the world-famous Pork Chop Sandwich, the go-to meal of locals and visitors alike. Visit Snappy Lunch today to sample Charles Dowell's creation.

**Monday – Wednesday & Friday: 5:45 am to 1:45 pm**
**Thursday & Saturday: 5:45 am to 1:15 pm**

# *Pork Chop Sandwich*

**10 (3.5-ounce) pork tenderloins**
**2 cups all-purpose flour**
**2 tablespoons sugar**
**Salt to taste**
**2 eggs, beaten**
**1 cup milk**
**Oil for frying**
**1 bun**
**Mustard, homemade chili and homemade slaw for dressing**
**Onion slices**
**Tomato slices**

Pound tenderloins with a meat mallet to tenderize; rinse and pat dry with paper towels. In a mixing bowl, combine flour, sugar and salt; stir in eggs. Slowly stir in milk, beating until batter is smooth (not lumpy or watery). In a skillet, preheat ½ inch oil to 350°. Generously dredge tenderloins in batter, then place in oil. Turn occasionally, cooking about 15 to 20 minutes or until loins are done. Drain on paper towels and slice. Serve pork chop slices on a warm bun dressed with mustard, chili, slaw, onion and tomato.

**Restaurant Recipe**

# River Wild

**1185 Lillys Bridge Road**
**Mount Gilead, NC 27306**
**910-439-2022**
**www.riverwildnc.com • Find us on Facebook**

Located on Lake Tillery, River Wild is a cabin-style restaurant that features onsite catering, local events, and delivery services. Relax by the Lilly's Bridge Marina while you wait on your table, taking in the beautiful lake and surrounding scenery. Sample appetizers, like oysters and crispy firecracker shrimp; fresh soups and salads, like bison chili and Asian ahi tuna salad; various sandwiches and handcrafted burgers, like po-boys and pimento burgers; delicious Korean barbecue tacos; chicken tender baskets; and fresh seafood, like tequila lime salmon, shrimp and grits, and fish 'n' chips. Times spent with friends and family at River Wild are always memorable and special.

**Monday – Thursday: 4:00 pm to 9:00 pm**
**Friday & Saturday: 11:00 am to 11:00 pm**
**Sunday: 11:00 am to 9:00 pm**

## *Country Biscuits*

**2 cups flour**
**1 tablespoon baking powder**
**1 teaspoon salt**
**¼ teaspoon baking soda**
**⅓ cup shortening**
**¾ cup buttermilk**

Preheat oven to 450°. Mix dry ingredients thoroughly. Cut in shortening with edge of spoon until mixture is crumbly. Add most of buttermilk and stir to mix. Add more buttermilk as needed to make a dough that is soft but not too sticky to knead. Knead dough on a lightly floured surface 10 to 12 times. Pat dough to ½-inch thickness. Cut with a floured biscuit cutter or cut into squares with a knife. Place 1 inch apart on a greased baking sheet for crusty biscuits or together for softer biscuits. Bake 12 to 15 minutes or until golden brown.

**Local Favorite**

## *Bouillon Gravy*

**1 tablespoon shortening**
**2 tablespoons flour**
**2 beef bouillon cubes, crumbled**
**Salt and pepper to taste**

Melt shortening in frying pan ovcr medium-low heat. Remove from heat and stir in flour, mixing well to make a smooth paste. Return to heat; cook until color changes to a light golden brown. Stir in 1 cup water, crumbled bouillon cubes, salt and pepper. Simmer to a smooth gravy consistency.

**Local Favorite**

**40 Chinquapin Road**
**Pinehurst, NC 28374**
**910-295-3193**
**www.drumandquill.com**
**Find us on Facebook**

Welcome to Drum & Quill Public House, home to golf's majors and golf's professional grand slam. "Drum" in the name honors the famous golf writer and Emmy-nominated broadcaster Bob Drum, while "Quill" represents the golf writer's pen, a secret weapon that turns stories into legends. Guests will enjoy appetizers, like pork barbecue nachos; house soups, like French onion soup; fresh salads, like fried green tomato caprese; tacos, like Korean beef tacos; gourmet burgers, like the Cali burger; pub sandwiches, like shrimp po-boys; dinner baskets; steak and more. Come enjoy great food at this humble pub in the heart of Old Town Pinehurst.

**Monday – Tuesday & Sunday:**
**11:30 am to 10:00 pm**
**Wednesday & Thursday:**
**11:30 am to 11:00 pm**
**Friday & Saturday: 11:30 am to 1:00 am**

## *Beef & Brie Sandwich*

**8 ounces roast beef, sliced**
**2 slices Tuscan bread**
**2 tablespoons butter**
**2 ounces Brie cheese**
**2 ounces Honeycup mustard**
**1 pickle spear**

In a skillet, cook roast beef until heated, making sure to leave a slight pink color; set aside. In another skillet, toast bread in butter. To assemble, place down 1 slice bread and top with half of beef. Top with Brie, then top with remaining beef. Pour mustard over top; top with last slice bread. Slice in half on a diagonal and plate neatly using a skewer. Serve with a pickle spear and your choice of side (chips, fries, wontons, etc.).

Restaurant Recipe

## *Monte Cristo Sandwich*

**3 ounces turkey, sliced**
**3 ounces ham, sliced**
**2 slices Tuscan bread**
**2 eggs, beaten**
**2 tablespoons butter**
**2 slices Swiss cheese**
**¼ cup raspberry dipping sauce**
**1 pickle spear**

In a skillet, cook turkey and ham until heated. Coat bread slices in egg. In a skillet, melt butter; cook bread, open-faced, in skillet with 1 slice cheese on each piece. When cheese is melted, place turkey on one slice and ham on other; press sandwich halves together, slice on a diagonal and plate neatly using a skewer. Serve with raspberry dipping sauce, a pickle spear and your choice of side (chips, fries, wontons, etc.).

Restaurant Recipe

# Lady Bedford's Tea Parlour & Gift Shoppe

**21 Chinquapin Road**
**Pinehurst, NC 28374**
**910-255-0100**
**www.ladybedfords.com • Find us on Facebook**

## *Kentucky Bourbon Bacon & Cheddar Quiche*

**1 (9-inch) deep-dish pie crust**
**4 large eggs**
**¾ cup milk**
**¾ cup heavy cream**
**⅛ teaspoon pepper**
**20 slices Kentucky bourbon bacon, cooked and crumbled**
**1½ cups shredded sharp Cheddar cheese**

Preheat oven to 375°. Bake crust 5 minutes; remove and set aside. In a small bowl, whisk together eggs, milk, cream and pepper; pour into crust. Sprinkle bacon and cheese over top. Bake 30 minutes or until quiche filling is set and lightly browned. Serves 6 to 8. Pair with a hearty breakfast tea, such as Assam Satrupa or English breakfast.

**Recipe by Executive Chef Joseph W. Henderson**

Located in the historic village of Pinehurst, Lady Bedford's Tea Parlour & Gift Shoppe is a Victorian-style tea parlour offering a unique change of pace if you're looking for a special breakfast, relaxing lunch, or elegant afternoon tea. Guests will dine in a Victorian atmosphere, replete with crystal, fine china, linen tablecloths, and napkins. Enjoy over sixty high-quality, loose-leaf teas, each brewed individually at the time of your order. The tea parlour offers a lunch menu with a selection of daily soups, salads, sandwiches, and desserts, along with a full afternoon tea menu, including scones with lemon curd, Devonshire cream, and fruit preserves. You're sure to find something to please your palate. Stop in for a cup of tea and Southern charm, Victorian-style.

**Tuesday – Saturday: 8:00 am to 4:00 pm**

## *Devonshire Cream*

**4 ounces cream cheese**
**4 ounces sour cream**
**2 cups heavy cream**
**2 teaspoons powdered sugar**
**1 teaspoon vanilla**

Using a stand mixer with a whisk attachment, mix all ingredients 5 minutes on high speed, until smooth. Makes 1½ quarts. Serve with scones.

**Recipe by Executive Chef Joseph W. Henderson**

## *Lemon Curd*

**1½ cups lemon juice**
**8 lemons, zested**
**8 eggs**
**3 cups granulated sugar**
**3 sticks unsalted butter**

In a saucepan over low heat, combine lemon juice and zest. Beat in eggs and sugar. Add butter. Cook, stirring constantly, until curd thickens. Strain immediately and cool. Serve with scones.

**Recipe by Executive Chef Joseph W. Henderson**

## *Cherry-Almond Scones*

**2 cups all-purpose flour**
**¼ cup granulated sugar**
**2 tablespoons baking powder**
**¼ teaspoon salt**
**5 ounces dried cherries, rehydrated**
**6 tablespoons butter, softened**
**1 egg**
**¼ cup milk**
**¼ cup heavy cream**
**1 teaspoon vanilla extract**
**2 teaspoons almond extract**

Preheat oven to 375°. In a stand mixer bowl, mix dry ingredients. In another bowl, whisk together wet ingredients; with stand mixer running, slowly add wet ingredients, taking care not to overmix. Turn out dough onto a floured surface, roll out to ½-inch thickness and cut out scones with a biscuit cutter. Arrange on a parchment-lined cookie sheet, then bake 12 minutes or until lightly browned. Makes about 16 scones.

**Recipe by Executive Chef Joseph W. Henderson**

# The Market Place Restaurant

**246 Olmsted Boulevard**
**Pinehurst, NC 28374**
**910-295-1160**
**www.themprestaurant.com • Find us on Facebook**

If you haven't been to The Market Place Restaurant, you don't know what you're missing. Having served their customers for more than 38 years, they've become quite the talk of the town. In fact, many of their customers visit regularly, so it's not uncommon to see a friendly face. Offering delicious food with Southern hospitality and a pleasant atmosphere, the overall experience is simply delightful. Enjoy gourmet sandwiches, soups, salads, and quiches. When you've built up a thirst, order the signature tea, lemonade, or soda. And don't forget about the best homemade desserts around. They also deliver and have a great space for private events in the evenings. The Market Place Restaurant is quite simply the place to be for lunch.

**Monday – Friday: 9:30 am to 2:30 pm**
**Saturday: 10:00 am to 2:00 pm**

## *Spiced Iced Tea*

**1 gallon-size tea bag**
**12 whole cloves**
**1 cup sugar, optional**

In a large stockpot, add tea bag, cloves and 1 quart water. Bring to a boil and remove from heat; let tea steep 1 hour. In a gallon jug, add sugar; pour prepared tea over top and stir until sugar dissolves. If desired, you may also leave out sugar to enjoy a delicious unsweetened tea. Leave cloves in, as they will sink to the bottom.

**Restaurant Recipe**

**75 West Salisbury Street**
**Pittsboro, NC 27312**
**919-704-8612**
**www.postalfishcompany.com • Find us on Facebook**

The Postal Fish Company is a Southern-Atlantic fish house restaurant located in the Piedmont of North Carolina. James and Bill have over forty years of combined cooking experience, having spent the last decade developing and learning about the underutilized bounty of North Carolina's coastal waters. Visit The Postal Fish Company and be drawn into a place where the sweet smells of the ocean flow through the air, and the sounds of blues to classic rock create the perfect atmosphere. The combination of a comfortable setting, top-notch service, and great food is sure to keep you coming back for a long time to come.

**Lunch:**
**Thursday – Saturday: 11:00 am to 2:00 pm**
**Dinner:**
**Tuesday – Thursday: 5:00 pm to 9:00 pm**
**Friday & Saturday: 5:00 pm to 10:00 pm**
**Brunch:**
**Sunday: 11:00 am to 2:00 pm**

## Crispy Fish Collars with Texas Pete Butter

**1 tablespoon onion powder**
**1 tablespoon garlic powder**
**1 tablespoon smoked paprika**
**1 tablespoon black pepper plus more**
**1½ tablespoons sea salt plus more**
**2 cups buttermilk**
**12 grouper collars, cleaned and patted dry**
**1½ cups Texas Pete hot sauce**
**1 cup packed brown sugar**
**½ pound butter**
**1 gallon peanut oil**
**1½ cups fine white cornmeal**
**2 cups flour**

In a bowl, blend all spices; whisk in buttermilk. Add collars to buttermilk mixture; marinate 2 hours or up to 2 days. In a saucepan, mix Texas Pete and brown sugar; simmer 3 to 4 minutes, then remove from heat and stir in butter. Keep warm. Preheat peanut oil in deep fryer to 365°. In a bowl, mix cornmeal, flour, salt and pepper to taste; roll collars in flour mixture, ensuring they are well coated. Fry 3 to 4 minutes or until they float. Drain on paper towels, toss in Texas Pete Butter and serve immediately.

**Restaurant Recipe**

## Wood-Grilled Peel-N-Eat Garlic Shrimp

**8 cloves garlic**
**Olive oil**
**1½ sticks butter, softened**
**1 teaspoon chili powder**
**1 teaspoon smoked paprika**
**2 teaspoons sea salt plus more**
**1 teaspoon black pepper plus more**
**3 tablespoons hot sauce**
**2 tablespoons Worcestershire sauce**
**¼ cup chopped parsley**
**24 large shrimp, unpeeled**
**1 lemon, sliced in wedges for garnish**

Coat 4 cloves garlic with olive oil; roast until golden brown, then mash into a paste with a fork. Mince remaining garlic and mix with paste. In a stand mixer, whip butter and garlic with spices, sauces and parsley until well mixed. With scissors, split shrimp up the back; devein. Pat dry, toss in oil and season with salt and pepper. Grill until shrimp have curled and turned pink. Place half of butter mixture in a bowl; place remaining butter in a sealable container in refrigerator for next batch. Remove shrimp from grill and quickly toss in garlic butter until it melts. Serve immediately with lemon wedges for garnish.

**Restaurant Recipe**

# Simply Better Seafood

**231 Flagstone Lane**
**Raeford, NC 28376**
**910-479-3520**
**www.simplybetterseafoodco.com • Find us on Facebook**

Simply Better Seafood is a veteran-owned and -operated wholesale seafood company that also runs Simply Better Seafood restaurant, market, and raw bar. The restaurant specializes in providing wholesale and retail customers with seafood of exceptional quality. Simply Better Seafood has a hand in the seafood it carries at every stage, from catch to plate. Enjoy seafood cooked any way you want it: sautéed, grilled, baked, broiled, steamed or raw by the ounce or pound. Pick it out of the seafood cases and let the kitchen staff prepare it for you or have it packed to take home. Simply Better Seafood does it better!

**Wednesday & Thursday: Noon to 9:00 pm**
**Friday & Saturday: Noon to 2:00 am**
**Sunday: Noon to 8:00 pm**

## *Beef Jerky*

**1 flank steak**
**Soy sauce**
**Garlic powder to taste**
**Hickory salt to taste**
**Lemon pepper to taste**

Cut steak into thin strips; add to a zip-close bag. Add enough soy sauce to bag to cover steak and marinate overnight. Remove steak from bag and arrange on a wire rack; sprinkle with garlic powder, hickory salt and lemon pepper. Bake at 150° for 15 hours or to desired dryness.

**Local Favorite**

## *Apple Sticky Buns*

**2 to 3 apples, sliced**
**½ cup packed brown sugar**
**2 teaspoons cinnamon**
**1 teaspoon nutmeg**
**1 (10-count) can biscuits**
**½ cup melted margarine**

Preheat oven to 350°. Arrange apple slices in bottom of greased 8-inch square baking dish. In a bowl, mix together brown sugar, cinnamon and nutmeg. Separate biscuits and coat with sugar mixture. Arrange coated biscuits over apple slices. Drizzle with margarine. Bake 20 to 30 minutes or until golden brown.

**Local Favorite**

## Clyde Cooper's Barbeque

**327 South Wilmington Street**
**Raleigh, NC 27601**
**919-832-7614**
**www.clydecoopersbbq.com**
**Find us on a Facebook**

Welcome to Clyde Cooper's Barbeque. Since 1938, Clyde Cooper's has been serving Eastern Carolina-style barbeque in Downtown Raleigh. Dig in to succulent, tender, slow-cooked barbeque made from only top-grade lean and clean pork shoulders. All that delicious flavor comes together perfectly when meshed with a splash of the custom-made, vinegar-based barbeque sauce. Be sure to go light so that you don't miss out on that tasty, smoky goodness. Combine kickin' barbeque with a whole lotta good hospitality, and you'll be hard-pressed to find a better barbeque joint in North Carolina. Stop by Clyde Cooper's Barbeque for good eating and friendly service.

**Monday – Saturday: 10:00 am to 6:00 pm**

## *Mac & Cheese*

**1 stick butter**
**1½ cups powdered chicken base, divided**
**5½ pounds pasta**
**¾ cup Texas Pete hot sauce**
**3 tablespoons coarse black pepper**
**3 (12-ounce) cans evaporated milk**
**4 cups grated jalapeño cheese**
**8 cups grated Cheddar cheese plus more for topping**

Preheat oven to 375°. In a 20-inch-diameter, heavy-bottomed stockpot, add 5½ gallons water, butter and ¾ cup chicken base; bring to a boil. Add pasta; boil 10 minutes or until al dente. Carefully drain off half the water; mix in remaining chicken base, hot sauce, pepper and milk. Add cheeses; mix until well combined. Adjust seasoning to taste. Transfer mixture to a greased 12x18-inch hotel pan; cover top with Cheddar cheese. Bake 1 hour or until a thermometer inserted into the middle reads 145°.

**Restaurant Recipe**

## *Cheerwine Baked Beans*

**2 gallons [about 2½ (96-ounce) cans] vegetarian baked beans in brown sugar, drained**
**¾ cup prepared mustard**
**6 cups Sweet Baby Ray's barbecue sauce**
**2 cups finely chopped yellow onion**
**2 cups finely chopped green bell pepper**
**2 cups Cheerwine soda**

Preheat oven to 375°. In a full-size hotel pan, mix together all ingredients. Taste and adjust balance of mustard, barbecue sauce and Cheerwine until you get the flavor you desire. You may also add more onion or bell pepper, if desired. Bake, uncovered, 1 hour or until thermometer inserted into middle reads 165°. Serves 25 to 30 people.

**Restaurant Recipe**

# Driftwood Southern Kitchen

**8460 Honeycutt Road, Suite 112**
**Raleigh, NC 27615**
**919-977-8360**
**www.driftwoodraleigh.com • Find us on Facebook**

Located in Lafayette Village, Driftwood Southern Kitchen is the latest addition to North Raleigh's blossoming local dining scene. Featuring a unique open kitchen, a communal-style, semi-private room, and a large open dining room, Driftwood offers a scratch-made menu that showcases the best ingredients from local farms and regional producers wherever possible. Born out of strong love for Southern ingredients and Southern hospitality, Driftwood showcases rustic farmhouse cooking at its finest. The restaurant is a little quirky with a touch of serious, but the staff put a lot of love into what they do. Visit Driftwood Southern Kitchen, create memories, and share a meal with the ones you love.

**Monday – Thursday: 11:00 am to 9:00 pm**
**Friday & Saturday: 11:00 am to 10:00 pm**
**Sunday: 4:30 pm to 8:30 pm**
**Brunch Buffet:**
**Sunday: 10:00 am to 2:00 pm**

## *Shrimp & Grits with Tomato-Andouille Beurre Blanc*

**4 cups milk**
**1⅜ cups heavy cream, divided**
**1 tablespoon chopped thyme, divided**
**¼ tablespoon granulated garlic**
**½ tablespoon salt plus more to taste**
**¼ tablespoon pepper plus more to taste**
**2 cups dry, local stone-ground grits**
**1 cup shredded Cheddar cheese**
**¼ pound unsalted butter**
**½ cup white wine**
**¼ cup diced shallots**
**½ pound butter**
**¼ cup diced Roma tomatoes**
**¼ cup diced andouille sausage**
**¼ lemon, juiced**
**2 dozen medium shrimp, peeled and deveined**
**2 tablespoons olive oil**

In a stockpot, bring 2 cups water, milk and 1 cup heavy cream to a boil. Add ¼ tablespoon thyme, garlic, salt and pepper. Reduce heat to low and whisk in grits; cook 30 minutes, stirring constantly. Remove from heat; stir in cheese and unsalted butter. Make Tomato-Andouille Beurre Blanc by adding wine, shallots and remaining thyme to a skillet over medium heat, cooking until reduced. Add remaining heavy cream, then reduce again. Stir in butter until melted. Remove from heat; add tomato, sausage and lemon juice. Adjust seasoning with salt and pepper to taste. In a skillet over medium heat, sauté shrimp in olive oil, seasoning with salt and pepper to taste; cook 2 minutes per side, then finish with Beurre Blanc. Plate grits and pour shrimp with sauce over top.

**Restaurant Recipe**

# J. Betski's

**10 West Franklin Street**
**Raleigh, NC 27604**
**919-833-7999**
**www.jbetskis.com • Find us on Facebook**

Established in 2006, J. Betski's accentuates owner John F. Korzekwinski's German and Polish heritage, offering a sampling of the delicious cuisine and fine beverages of Central and Eastern Europe. The menu preparation emphasizes the use of quality ingredients, with many being sourced from local farms. The warm and inviting design of the bar and dining areas provide you with the ideal setting for an escape to the Old World here in the New South. Dine on potato and cheese pierogies, pastrami sliders, pork schnitzel sandwiches, fresh kielbasa on a toasted roll, and so much more. Visit Seaboard Station in Downtown Raleigh, where you'll find J. Betski's waiting to serve you.

**Lunch:**
**Tuesday – Friday: 11:30 am to 2:00 pm**
**Saturday: 11:30 am to 2:30 pm**
**Dinner:**
**Tuesday – Saturday: 5:30 pm to 10:00 pm**

## *Sliced Candied Potatoes*

**4 large sweet potatoes, peeled and thinly sliced**
**1 cup light brown sugar**
**1 cup white sugar**
**2½ tablespoons flour**
**Dash salt**
**4 tablespoons butter, melted**
**1 teaspoon lemon flavoring**

Preheat oven to 350°. Place potatoes in a buttered 9x13-inch baking dish. Mix sugars with flour and salt; sprinkle over potatoes. Combine butter with lemon flavoring and drizzle over top. Add ½ cup hot water to allow potatoes to cook. Bake 30 minutes or until potatoes are tender and candied.

**Local Favorite**

## *Corn Pudding*

**1 (15-ounce) can cream-style corn**
**1 (15-ounce) can whole-kernel corn, drained**
**1 tablespoon sugar**
**1 teaspoon flour**
**2 tablespoons butter**
**1 egg, slightly beaten**
**⅓ cup evaporated milk**

Preheat oven to 350°. In a bowl, mix all ingredients; pour into a greased 1-quart baking dish. Bake 10 minutes or until firm.

**Local Favorite**

**1130 Buck Jones Road**
**Raleigh, NC 27606**
**919-380-0122**
**www.reysrestaurant.com • Find us on Facebook**

Founded in 2004 with the vision of quality, owner A. Rey Arias thought that if Rey's Restaurant never compromised the quality of its food and strove to serve meals in a comfortable, relaxed surrounding with warm, friendly service that people would keep coming back. Well, it worked! Accordingly, the restaurant never changed its vision. Arias gave his name to the restaurant out of a sincere sense of pride and confidence in the menu and staff. Rey's Restaurant pledges to maintain high-quality standards, so it can continue to enjoy your valued patronage again and again. The staff at Rey's Restaurant look forward to showing you a fabulous dining experience.

**Monday – Thursday: 5:00 pm to 10:00 pm**
**Friday & Saturday: 5:00 pm to 11:00 pm**

**Private Dining Available for Parties of 6 to 300**

## *Creamed Spinach*

**1 pound butter**

**½ cup olive oil**

**4 Vidalia onions, minced**

**½ cup minced garlic**

**4 (2-pound) packages spinach, stemmed and chopped**

**2 tablespoons each salt and freshly ground black pepper**

**1 tablespoon freshly ground nutmeg**

**2 quarts heavy cream**

**1 quart half-and-half**

**1 cup flour**

In a medium skillet over medium-high heat, melt butter and add olive oil. Add onion and garlic; sauté 2 minutes until soft. Add spinach and warm through (wilt). Add salt, pepper, nutmeg and heavy cream; mix well and bring to a boil. Whisk in half-and-half and flour; cook over medium-high heat 3 to 4 minutes or until liquid is reduced by half.

**Restaurant Recipe**

## *Rey's Chocolate Raspberry Truffle Cake*

**2 tablespoons butter plus more for buttering dish**

**1 stick unsalted butter**

**¾ pound semi-sweet chocolate chips**

**¼ pound unsweetened chocolate, chopped**

**1 pound sugar**

**4 ounces raspberry Melba sauce**

**½ cup brewed coffee**

**4 eggs**

**1 teaspoon vanilla extract**

Preheat oven to 300°. Butter a 9-inch cake pan and line with parchment. Add butters to a saucepan and bring to a boil, then remove from heat. Stir in chocolates until melted; do not overmix or air bubbles will form. Transfer chocolate mixture to a bowl with sugar, Melba sauce and coffee; mix slowly until blended. Stir in eggs and vanilla; pour into prepared pan. Fill a roasting pan three-quarters full with water; place cake pan inside. Bake 1 hour. Cake should jiggle when done. If too soft, bake 10 minutes more. Let sit 2 hours at room temperature. Cover with plastic wrap and refrigerate overnight.

**Restaurant Recipe**

# 24 Blackbirds Café & Market

**209 Southwest Market Street**
**Reidsville, NC 27320**
**336-394-4363**
**www.24blackbirdscatering.com**
**Find us on Facebook**

Welcome to 24 Blackbirds Café & Market, a café and catering service inspired by the belief that delicious food is the key to any successful event. At 24 Blackbirds, customers' needs are of the utmost importance, as is making sure every guest is happy. The entire team is committed to exceeding your expectations and preparing fantastic food. The café serves lunch during the week, and the space is also available for private events. Catering is available for events big and small, including private functions, corporate event catering, weddings and everything in between. You'll experience superior service with genuine enthusiasm every time.

**Monday – Friday: 11:00 am to 3:00 pm**
**Saturday & Sunday by Appointment**

## *Picnic Potato Salad*

**5 pounds red potatoes**
**2 tablespoons Dijon mustard**
**2 cups mayonnaise**
**2 cups sour cream**
**1 tablespoon chopped fresh dill**
**3 tablespoons chopped fresh parsley**
**1 cup diced celery**
**½ red onion, diced**
**3 teaspoons kosher salt**
**1 teaspoon fresh ground pepper**

Chop potatoes, leaving peels on; place in a large saucepan, cover with water and bring to a boil. Cook potatoes until fork-tender; remove from heat and drain. Cool potatoes 20 minutes, then add mustard, mayonnaise and sour cream. Fold in remaining ingredients until well combined. Chill before serving. Makes 20 to 25 servings.

**Restaurant Recipe**

## PATTAN'S DOWNTOWN GRILLE

**228 A East Washington Street**
**Rockingham, NC 28379**
**910-895-8080**
**www.pattansdowntowngrille.com**
**Find us on Facebook**

Pattan's Downtown Grille is a full-service restaurant featuring the award-winning barbecue of Tim Pattan. The restaurant offers a variety of rotating daily specials. Try tasty rib-eye sandwiches on Tuesdays, "Burnt Ends" brisket dishes on Wednesdays, chicken dishes on Thursday, shrimp dishes on Fridays, and ribs on Saturdays afternoons. You may also order from the regular menu, which is replete with salads, soups, sandwich specials, burgers, platters, tacos, and tasty sides. Don't forget to try the one-of-a-kind Pee Dee River Swamp Sauce, great served over barbecue or on the Pattan special sandwich. Finish with a homemade dessert, like the cinnamon bun cheesecake, for the complete Pattan's dining experience.

**Tuesday – Thursday: 11:00 am to 8:30 pm**
**Friday & Saturday: 11:00 am to 9:00 pm**

## *Swamp Dip*

**1 pound ground beef**
**1 pound breakfast sausage**
**½ cup finely diced onion**
**½ cup finely diced green bell pepper**
**1 pound Velveeta cheese, small-cubed**
**16 ounces Pee Dee River Swamp Sauce**
**Tortilla chips**

In a saucepan over medium heat, brown meats and sauté vegetables, breaking meat into small pieces as it cooks; drain excess grease. Add cheese and Swamp Sauce. Cook over low heat until cheese is melted. Serve with your favorite tortilla chips.

**Restaurant Recipe**

## *Basic Meat Rub*

**¾ cup paprika**
**½ cup packed brown sugar**
**½ cup salt**
**¼ cup ground black pepper**
**2 tablespoons dried thyme**
**2 tablespoons dry mustard**
**1 tablespoon ground cumin**
**1 tablespoon cayenne pepper**
**1 tablespoon ground sage**

In a bowl, whisk together all ingredients until combined, making sure that brown sugar is not clumped. Use on beef, pork, chicken or seafood before grilling or baking. Store in an airtight container when not in use.

**Restaurant Recipe**

# Firehouse Foods

**400 Southtown Circle**
**Rolesville, NC 27571**
**919-435-1520**
**www.firehousefoods.org • Find us on Facebook**

Welcome to Firehouse Foods. Owned and operated by a team of public safety workers, Firehouse was opened in February 2018 by Lee Price, executive chef turned firefighter, and his wife, Aelisch. In his youth, Lee learned to cook working in restaurants, perfecting his craft at Amos Mosquito's in Atlantic Beach. As a firefighter, Lee cooked meals for his coworkers and other personnel but still dreamed of opening a restaurant. Now Lee, Aelisch, and EMS medics Matt and Summer Masters bring you a new, exciting experience. Firehouse Foods serves made-to-order meals, sauces, dressings, pimento cheese, chicken salad, and more. From burgers to prime rib, cookies to milkshakes, they've got you covered.

**Monday – Saturday: 7:00 am to 8:30 pm**
**Sunday: 7:00 am to 3:00 pm**

## *Mom's Firehouse Homemade Pancakes*

**1 cup self-rising flour**
**⅓ cup vegetable oil**
**1 large egg**
**1 pinch sugar**
**1 teaspoon vanilla extract**
**1 cup milk or to desired consistency**

Mix flour, oil, egg, sugar, and vanilla with milk in a bowl. Do not use mixer; use hand whisk. (If you use a mixer, pancakes will be flat rather than fluffy.) Makes 4 to 6 medium-size pancakes.

**Restaurant Recipe**

## *Firehouse Homemade Ranch Dressing*

**2 cups sour cream**
**1 cup Duke's mayonnaise**
**1 tablespoon Lawry's garlic salt**
**1 teaspoon white pepper**
**½ cup chopped parsley**
**1 teaspoon lemon juice**
**Buttermilk to consistency**

Mix sour cream, mayonnaise and garlic salt together. Add in white pepper, parsley and lemon juice. Mix in buttermilk until desired consistency is reached.

**Restaurant Recipe**

# Brookland Eats

**333 Old Durham Road**
**Roxboro, NC 27573**
**336-322-1015**
**www.brooklandeats.com**
**Find us on Facebook & Instagram**

BROOKLAND EATS
EST. 2013
ROXBORO, NC.

Originally opened in 2013, Brookland Eats proudly serves the locals of Person County and the surrounding counties. Choosing fresh ingredients from many local farms, Brookland Eats offers a variety of fresh American-style, handmade dishes. The interior boasts the rustic sensibilities of Roxboro, while also paying tribute to Person County's storied past. The restaurant is owned and operated by Chef David Gaydeski, who served for nearly a decade as executive chef to three governors at the North Carolina executive mansion in Raleigh. Chef David graduated from the International Culinary Academy and has worked for Hyatt Regency hotels, restaurants, and country clubs across North Carolina. Enjoy a fresh, delicious meal at Brookland Eats today.

Lunch:
**Tuesday – Saturday: 11:00 am to 2:30 pm**
Dinner:
**Tuesday – Saturday: 5:00 pm to 9:00 pm**
Brunch:
**Sunday: 10:30 am to 2:30 pm**

## *Braised Greens*

**8 ounces smoked bacon, chopped**

**¼ cup olive oil**

**2 tablespoons chopped garlic**

**1 to 2 heads romaine lettuce, washed and chopped**

**1 to 2 cups chicken stock**

**2 to 3 tablespoons grated Parmesan cheese**

**Red pepper flakes to taste**

**Salt and pepper to taste**

In a large skillet or heavy-bottom stockpot over medium heat, add bacon; cook until crispy. Remove bacon from skillet and set aside; add oil and reduce heat to medium low. Add garlic; cook until aromatic, taking care not to brown it. Add lettuce and stock to skillet. Crumble bacon and add back to skillet; simmer 5 minutes. Greens may look soupy, but that's okay. Add Parmesan, red pepper flakes, salt and pepper. Cook until cheese melts and serve. Makes about 6 servings.

**Restaurant Recipe**

## *Chef's Favorite Crab Cakes*

**Oil for frying**

**3 pounds lump crabmeat**

**1 pound jumbo lump crabmeat**

**1½ cups mayonnaise**

**1 cup breadcrumbs**

**2 tablespoons Old Bay seasoning**

**2 tablespoons garlic powder**

**1 tablespoon onion powder**

**2 lemons, zested**

**¼ cup olive oil**

**1 tablespoon Dijon mustard**

**4 whole eggs**

In a skillet over medium-high heat, preheat frying oil. Preheat oven to 350°. In a large bowl, mix together remaining ingredients until well combined. Form mixture into patties; add to preheated oil. Sear on one side 2 minutes. Remove patties from oil and place, seared side up, on a parchment-lined cookie sheet. Finish by baking Crab Cakes 10 minutes.

**Restaurant Recipe**

# Troyer's Country Market

**4077 Statesville Boulevard**
**Salisbury, NC 28147**
**704-637-0733**
**www.troyersmarketnc.com • Find us on Facebook**

In his youth, JR Troyer watched his Mennonite uncles working bulk food stores they owned and managed in separate states, including one in Blanch. Though far apart in location, he saw that his uncles had a love of people and generous hearts. These values defined their stores and, eventually, the purpose behind JR's own dream. Many years later the opportunity arose for JR to start his own store. With prayer, he and his wife, Rebekah, opened Troyer's Country Market in June 2013, and five years later the store is still going strong. JR and Rebekah's goal is to establish a place of love and peace with the best fried doughnuts.

**Monday – Saturday: 9:00 am to 5:00 pm**
**Deli closes at 4:30 pm**

## *Scalloped Oysters*

**2 cups crushed Ritz crackers (or other butter-flavored crackers)**
**½ cup melted butter**
**Dash black pepper**
**½ teaspoon salt**
**1 pint shucked oysters**
**1 cup heavy cream**
**¼ teaspoon Worcestershire sauce**

Preheat oven to 350°. In a bowl, combine crackers, butter, pepper and salt. Spread a third of cracker mixture in the bottom of a greased 1½-quart baking dish. Arrange half of oysters over cracker mixture. Top with another third cracker mixture. Layer remaining oysters over cracker mixture. In a bowl, combine Worcestershire and cream; pour over top of oysters. Top with remaining third of cracker mixture. Bake, uncovered, 30 to 40 minutes or until top is golden brown.

**Restaurant Recipe**

## *Dried Beef Cheese Ball*

**1 tablespoon Worcestershire sauce**
**¼ medium onion, grated**
**3 (8-ounce) packages cream cheese, softened**
**1 tablespoon Accent Flavor Enhancer seasoning**
**1 cup grated dried beef**
**Snack crackers for serving**

In a bowl, mix Worcestershire, onion, cream cheese and seasoning until well combined; roll into a ball. Place dried beef in another bowl, then roll Cheese Ball in beef to coat. Chill in an airtight container until set. Serve with snack crackers.

**Restaurant Recipe**

**146 South 3rd Street**
**Smithfield, NC 27577**
**919-205-1076**
**www.sodosopa.biz • Find us on Facebook**

With a name inspired by an episode of Comedy Central's hit series South Park, SoDoSoPa serves up elevated barbecue in a fun, casual atmosphere. Whether it's from Tennessee, Texas, Georgia, Louisiana, or the Carolinas, Southern barbecue is the sweetest taste around. SoDoSoPa's comfort food is sure to satisfy any appetite. Smoked brisket, pork, ribs, and chicken leg quarters are cooked low and slow for several hours to ensure that they melt in your mouth. The restaurant uses recipes gathered over six generations, across three families with strong roots in the South and its tradition of barbecue and soul food. Bring the whole family and experience down-home cooking for yourself.

**Monday – Saturday: 11:00 am to 9:00 pm**

## *Pepper Relish*

**2 red bell peppers, julienned**
**1 yellow onion, julienned**
**1 cup apple cider vinegar**
**1 tablespoon roasted garlic purée**
**½ cup sugar**
**¼ cup whole-grain mustard**

In a saucepan over medium heat, sauté peppers and onion until golden brown. Add remaining ingredients, then reduce heat to low. Heat until relish starts to thicken, stirring frequently.

**Restaurant Recipe**

## *Hog Cakes*

**2 cups diced red bell pepper**
**1 cup chopped green onion**
**3 cups mayonnaise**
**2 cups Dijon mustard**
**1 quart chopped pulled pork**
**2 quarts breadcrumbs**
**1 cup pasteurized eggs**

In a large mixing bowl, add bell pepper, onion, mayonnaise and mustard; mix together until combined. Fold in pulled pork, then add breadcrumbs; work together. Lastly, blend in pasteurized eggs. Refrigerate 1 hour. Using a 1-ounce scoop, scoop mixture and form into a hockey-puck-shaped cake. Deep fry 3 to 5 minutes at 350° or until golden brown. Serve with a garnish of Pepper Relish.

**Restaurant Recipe**

# Sweet Basil Café

**134 Northwest Broad Street**
**Southern Pines, NC 28387**
**910-693-1487**

Established in 1996 by John Davis and Pepi Brown, Sweet Basil Café has stood the test of time, serving Pepi's homemade soups and John's lunch creations for 22 years. Guests will enjoy a range of sandwiches made with house-made bread, baked fresh each morning by John. With favorites like the Smoked Turkey Melt, the Hot Vegetarian, and the Grilled Chicken Napa, you'll always leave wanting more. Pepi's homemade soups are the best in town. In addition to sandwiches and soups, the café also offers salads, pastas, and even pizza options. Visit on a Friday or Saturday for a chance to try John's mini cookies at the hostess stand.

**Tuesday – Saturday: 11:00 am to 3:00 pm**

## *Broccoli-Cheddar Chowder*

**1 cup chopped celery**
**1 cup chopped carrots**
**½ cup chopped onion**
**1 pound fresh broccoli, washed and chopped**
**1 stick butter**
**½ cup all-purpose flour**
**2 teaspoons salt**
**¼ teaspoon white pepper**
**4 cups milk**
**Hot pepper sauce to taste, optional**
**4 cups shredded Cheddar cheese**
**2 cups ½-inch-cubed, cooked ham**
**2 cups ½-inch-cubed, cooked potatoes**

In a large saucepan over medium heat, combine 2 cups water with celery, carrots, onion and broccoli; bring to a boil and cook 5 minutes or until tender. Do not drain. In a large saucepan, melt butter. Stir in flour, salt and pepper; cook, stirring constantly, 1 minute. Stir in milk, cooking until mixture thickens. Add hot pepper sauce, if desired. Stir in cheese until melted. Stir in ham and potatoes. Stir into undrained vegetables and warm through over medium-low heat, if needed. Enjoy.

**Restaurant Recipe**

## *Chicken Tortilla Soup*

**1 (14.5-ounce) can peeled Italian tomatoes, juice reserved**
**3 tablespoons vegetable oil plus more for frying**
**1 whole boneless, skinless chicken breast, halved**
**1 medium onion, chopped**
**3 cloves garlic, minced**
**2 teaspoons chili powder**
**2 teaspoons ground cumin**
**6 cups chicken stock**
**1 tablespoon tomato paste**
**1 (4-ounce) can chopped mild green chiles, drained**
**1 tablespoon deseeded and minced jalapeño peppers**
**4 corn tortillas, cut into ½-inch-wide strips**
**2 tablespoons chopped cilantro**
**Salt and pepper to taste**
**2 tablespoons grated Parmesan cheese**

In a food processor or blender, purée tomatoes with juices until smooth. In a large saucepan over medium heat, add 2 tablespoons oil; add chicken and cook 3 minutes each side or until golden brown. Transfer chicken to a plate, then heat remaining 1 tablespoon oil in saucepan; add onion and cook 5 minutes or until golden, stirring frequently. Add garlic, chili powder and cumin; cook 1 minute, stirring frequently. Add stock, puréed tomatoes, tomato paste, chiles and jalapeño. Return chicken to saucepan and bring to boil; reduce heat to low, cover and simmer 20 minutes. Remove chicken, cut into strips and return to saucepan. In a large skillet, heat ½ inch vegetable oil over medium-high heat. Add tortilla strips in batches and cook, stirring frequently, 1 to 2 minutes or until crisp. Transfer tortilla strips to a paper-towel-lined plate. Skim surface of soup, then stir in cilantro. Season with salt and pepper to taste. Divide tortilla strips among soup bowls and ladle soup over top. Serve sprinkled with Parmesan.

**Restaurant Recipe**

**155 Hall Avenue**
**Southern Pines, NC 28387**
**910-684-8758**
**www.thymeandplacecafe.com • Find us on Facebook**

The brainchild of owner Leslie Philip, Thyme & Place Café is a combination of a restaurant, marketplace, and communal kitchen that Leslie, a baker herself, would have been thrilled to have access to when she and her husband moved to Moore County. After twenty-five years in large-scale food manufacturing, Leslie decided the next step in her career was working on a smaller, local scale with community outreach. Guests will enjoy a full-service café with a licensed kitchen, where food entrepreneurs can make, market, and sell their products. The café even offers catering. In Thyme & Place Café, a brunch-and-lunch eatery meets kitchen entrepreneurship to fulfill a true need for the surrounding talented, agricultural community.

**Tuesday – Saturday: 10:00 am to 2:00 pm**

## *Widowed Potatoes*

**3 tablespoons olive oil**
**1 medium green bell pepper, medium diced**
**1 medium onion, medium diced**
**1 cup canned diced tomatoes, plus juices**
**3 pounds russet or Yukon Gold potatoes, peeled and cut into 1-inch chunks**
**1 head garlic, roasted and puréed**
**1 bay leaf**
**2 teaspoon salt**
**1 teaspoon smoked Spanish paprika**
**Freshly ground black pepper to taste**
**1 (8-ounce) can sardines, drained**

In a Dutch oven over medium heat, add oil. Add bell pepper and onion; sauté, stirring often, about 7 minutes or until softened. Add tomatoes, potatoes, garlic purée, bay leaf, salt, paprika, black pepper and 2 cups water; bring to a boil, and then reduce heat to medium low. Cover and cook 45 minutes or until vegetables are tender, stirring occasionally. Add sardines. Stir until heated through. Serve warm.

**Restaurant Recipe**

## *Ruby-Red Cabbage*

**1 large (2.5- to 3.5-pound) head red cabbage**
**2 tablespoons unsalted butter**
**1 cup dried cranberries or cherries**
**¼ cup red currant jelly (or apple jelly or apple juice)**
**1 tablespoon dark brown sugar**
**¼ cup red wine vinegar**
**Salt and pepper to taste**

Preheat oven to 350°. Wash and slice cabbage into thin strips; set aside. In a large, oven-safe pot over medium heat, melt butter. Add cranberries; cook 2 minutes or until berries begin to soften, stirring occasionally. Add cabbage and remaining ingredients. Reduce to low heat and cook 5 to 7 minutes or until cabbage is wilted, stirring occasionally. Cover pot and place in oven 1 hour. Serve hot or cold. Enjoy.

**Restaurant Recipe**

# Rock Store Bar-B-Q

**3116 Old Monroe Road**
**Stallings, NC 28104**
**704-821-0668**
**www.rockstorebbq.com • Find us on Facebook**

After decades as the only gasoline-service station for miles around (opened circa 1936), this unique landmark building continued to serve the tight-knit community of Stallings as a small convenience store. It became popularly well known to locals as "The Rock Store." Today, this humble little shop prides itself in serving up a slice of wood-smoked barbecue heaven to all who stop by. Whether you're looking for baby back ribs or a juicy barbecue sandwich, this charming cottage-style eatery has it all. Stallings Rock Store Bar-B-Q invites you and yours to visit sometime for a taste of that smoky Carolina 'cue.

**Monday – Saturday: 10:00 am to 7:30 pm**

## *Banana Pudding*

**1 gallon milk**
**2½ pounds sour cream**
**1 (8-ounce) container whipped topping**
**3½ cups vanilla pudding**
**Vanilla wafer cookies for layering**
**Sliced bananas for layering**

In a large bowl, mix milk, sour cream, whipped topping and vanilla pudding thoroughly. In a 9x13-inch dish, layer wafers and bananas until just shy of top; pour pudding mixture over top. Refrigerate until chilled throughout. Enjoy.

**Restaurant Recipe**

## *Red Slaw*

**1 cup sugar**
**1 cup white vinegar**
**1 teaspoon cayenne powder**
**1 teaspoon salt**
**2 cups diced tomatoes**
**1 cup diced red peppers**
**¾ cup sweet relish**
**5 pounds cabbage, shredded**

In a sealable bowl, toss together all ingredients until thoroughly mixed. Close lid and refrigerate at least 24 hours before serving.

**Restaurant Recipe**

## *Southern Brunswick Stew*

**1 cup rice**
**1 pound smoked meat (chicken, pork and beef)**
**2 tablespoons butter**
**48 ounces crushed tomatoes**
**27 ounces whole-kernel corn**
**8 ounces lima beans**
**¼ cup onion powder**
**2 tablespoons sugar**
**1 teaspoon pepper**
**1 teaspoon salt**
**1½ teaspoons Chili-O seasoning**

In a large stockpot, combine all ingredients plus 3½ cups water; set to low heat and cook 6 to 8 hours, making sure that a thermometer inserted into meat reads as least 165°. Enjoy.

**Restaurant Recipe**

# Homestead Steakhouse

**205 Frank Timberlake Road**
**Timberlake, NC 27583**
**336-364-8506**
**www.thehomesteadsteakhousenc.com • Find us on Facebook**

When you're hungry, don't settle for fast food. Dine at Homestead Steakhouse and enjoy flavorful dishes made from the freshest ingredients available. Homestead proudly serves certified Angus beef steaks. Highly trained chefs prepare your steak with a secret blend of spices, then chargrill it just the way you like it. Craving some great seafood? From deviled crabs to salmon steaks, Homestead has you covered. Traditional American cooking is what Homestead does best. Get your fill with the affordable homemade buffets. Enjoy decadent desserts that are sure to please your sweet tooth. Whether you desire meats, salads, or sweets, the buffet has it. Stop by the best steakhouse in town!

**Tuesday – Thursday: 5:00 pm to 9:00 pm**
**Friday: 5:00 pm to 9:30 pm**
**Saturday: 4:00 pm to 9:30 pm**
**Sunday: 11:30 am to 8:30 pm**

## *Homestead Southern Buttermilk Pie*

**½ cup buttermilk**
**1¾ cup sugar**
**2 large eggs**
**3 tablespoons flour**
**Pinch salt**
**½ cup melted butter**
**1 teaspoon vanilla extract**
**1 teaspoon nutmeg**
**1 (9-inch) deep-dish frozen pie crust, thawed**

Preheat oven to 400°. In a bowl, mix all ingredients until combined. Pour into a pie crust; sprinkle top with nutmeg. Bake 15 minutes. Reduce oven to 350°; bake 45 minutes. Cool to allow filling to set.

**Restaurant Recipe**

# Julia's Talley House Restaurant

**305 North Main Street #21**
**Troutman, NC 28166**
**704-528-69692**
**www.talleyhouse.net • Find us on Facebook**

Opened in 1979, Julia's Talley House prides itself on serving the Troutman community for decades. Julia and her son, Joe, began serving traditional Southern cuisine to good people at reasonable prices. Both Julia and Joe have since passed on, but Joe's wife, Kim, and her children and nephew Chris still carry on the multi-generational management of the restaurant's day-to-day operations. The restaurant happily provides the highest quality fried chicken, along with many other Southern favorites. Enjoy your meal either cafeteria- or family-style, the latter sure to rival the Sunday dinners of anyone's grandmother. The team at Julia's remembers what Southern hospitality used to feel like, and they want to remind you.

Lunch:
**Sunday – Friday: 11:00 am to 2:00 pm**
Dinner:
**Monday – Saturday: 5:00 pm to 8:30 pm**

## *Hershey's Pound Cake*

**3 cups sugar**
**2 sticks margarine**
**5 eggs**
**3½ cups all-purpose flour**
**½ teaspoon baking powder**
**½ teaspoon salt**
**1 cup milk**
**16 ounces Hershey's chocolate syrup**
**1 teaspoon vanilla extract**

Preheat oven to 325°. Grease and flour pound cake pan; set aside. Using a stand mixer, cream together sugar and margarine. Add eggs 1 at a time, beating after each addition. In a bowl, sift together flour, baking powder and salt; set aside. In another bowl, mix together milk, chocolate syrup and vanilla. Alternately add flour mixture and liquid mixture to creamed mixture, mixing well after each addition. Pour into prepared pan. Bake 1½ hours.

**Family Favorite**

## *Coconut Pie*

**1 cup flaked coconut**
**1 cup sugar**
**1 teaspoon vanilla extract**
**1½ cups milk**
**3 eggs, beaten**
**Pinch salt**
**2 tablespoons melted margarine**
**1 (9-inch) frozen pie shell, thawed**

Preheat oven to 325°. In a large bowl, combine all ingredients; mix well. Pour into pie shell and bake 45 minutes or until set.

**Restaurant Recipe**

# Real McCoys

**3325 Rogers Road**
**Wake Forest, NC 27587**
**919-562-8368**
**www.realmccoysnc.com • Find us on Facebook**

Real McCoys is more than just a restaurant; it's a community where customers are family. From top to bottom, the team at Real McCoys works together to provide you with an outstanding meal, the best craft beer selection in town, and a personal approach to service by which guests are made to feel right at home. The mission of Real McCoys is to create a space within the community where friends and families gather together, where memories are made over a hand-crafted meal; to support local musicians and breweries; and to harbor an environment where everyone is your neighbor. Visit Real McCoys for good folks, good food, and good times.

**Sunday – Thursday: 11:00 am to midnight**
**Friday & Saturday: 11:00 am to 2:00 am**

## *North Carolina BBQ Sauce*

**4 quarts ketchup**
**1 gallon apple cider vinegar**
**4 ounces red pepper flakes**
**3 ounces finely ground black pepper**
**1 (32-ounce) bag brown sugar**

In a saucepan over medium heat, whisk together all ingredients. Bring to a bubbling simmer, then reduce heat to low. Cook 10 minutes or until thickened, stirring occasionally. Enjoy with pork rinds or your favorite barbecue dish.

**Restaurant Recipe**

## *Real Bloody Mary Mix*

**1 (64-ounce) bottle V8 tomato juice**
**1 cup Worcestershire sauce**
**½ cup A1 steak sauce**
**4 tablespoons Old Bay seasoning**
**1 tablespoon packed brown sugar**
**1 tablespoon celery seed**
**6 tablespoons Texas Pete hot sauce**
**2 tablespoon freshly squeeze lime juice**

Add all ingredients to a food processor. Blend until combined.

**Restaurant Recipe**

**219 South White Street**
**Wake Forest, NC 27587**
**919-435-4436**
**www.sugarmagnoliacafe.com • Find us on Facebook**

"Local," "fresh," and "inviting" are perfect ways to describe Sugar Magnolia Café & Emporium. Located in the heart of the historic district of Downtown Wake Forest, Sugar Magnolia is a charming café, art emporium, and live music venue, all rolled into one place that feels as comfortable as your favorite chair and as inviting as the company of your best friend. Discover more than thirty-five artists and artisans while you enjoy freshly prepared dishes, like homemade pimento cheese, garden salads, or a variety of sandwiches, from ham and cheddar to the classic roasted turkey. Come see where food, art, and music all come together.

**Tuesday: 10:00 am to 5:00 pm**
**Wednesday – Thursday: 10:00 am to 9:00 pm**
**Friday – Saturday: 10:00 am to 10:00 pm**
**Sunday: Noon to 5:00 pm**

## *Devonshire Cream*

**1 pint heavy whipping cream**
**1 (8-ounce) package cream cheese, softened**
**¼ cup powdered sugar**
**1 teaspoon vanilla extract**

In a stand mixer, whip cream until dull and stiff, taking care not to over-whip. Add cream cheese, sugar and vanilla; whip on low speed until combined. Cover and refrigerate. Serve with scones.

**Restaurant Recipe**

## *Chocolate Chip Scones*

**3 cups all-purpose flour**
**½ cup sugar**
**1 teaspoon baking powder**
**¼ teaspoon salt**
**1 stick butter**
**2 eggs**
**½ cup milk**
**6 ounces chocolate chips**

Preheat oven to 400°. In a bowl, combine dry ingredients; cut in butter. Make a well in center of dry mixture; mix eggs and milk and add to well. Fold dry ingredients into wet until well blended. Fold in chocolate chips. Scoop onto a silicone-mat- or parchment-lined baking sheet with a large ice cream scoop; press down slightly. Bake 8 to 12 minutes. Cool, top with Devonshire Cream and serve with a pot of your favorite tea.

**Restaurant Recipe**

**111 North Bragg Street**
**Warrenton, NC 27589**
**252-257-1991**
**www.robinsonferrywarrenton.com • Find us on Facebook**

Right off Main Street, in a remodeled historic building, you will discover the best food, drink, and service between Raleigh and Richmond. At Robinson Ferry Restaurant & Spirits, it's all about the food. From local producers to steadfast suppliers, Robinson Ferry introduces ingredients to the kitchen that motivate chefs to create exciting recipes. From fresh whole fish to fresh-picked shiitake mushrooms, the right inspiration is key to creating a stunning dish. And you can't forget the drinks. With a bar featuring handcrafted cocktails, craft beer, and wine, you'll find the perfect pick-me-up to suit your taste. Come out to Robinson Ferry, where you'll be greeted with smiles, Southern hospitality, and outstanding service.

**Lunch:**
**Wednesday – Saturday: 11:00 am to 2:00 pm**
**Dinner:**
**Wednesday & Thursday: 5:00 pm to 9:00 pm**
**Friday & Saturday: 5:00 pm to 10:00 pm**

## *Cranberry Relish*

**1 cup pineapple juice**
**2 cups cranberry juice**
**1 cup key lime juice**
**3 cups red wine vinegar**
**1 red onion, finely diced**
**3 cups corn syrup**
**½ cup salt**
**8 cups dried cranberries**
**6 cups sugar, divided**
**4 cups sweet pickle relish**

In a saucepan, bring all ingredients except 4 cups sugar and pickle relish to a simmer. Stir in 4 cups sugar. Simmer until syrup-like consistency is achieved. Stir in sweet pickle relish. Serve over grilled pork chops, smoked turkey, stuffed chicken with bleu cheese or as part of a cheese and meat spread.

**Restaurant Recipe**

## *Smoked Tomato Vinaigrette*

**6 cups hickory-smoked, peeled Roma tomatoes**
**2 ½ cups white balsamic vinegar**
**1 tablespoon sugar**
**1 cup sunflower oil**

In a blender, process all ingredients except sunflower oil. Slowly blend in sunflower oil. Serve over salads, as a barbecue sauce for beef brisket or alongside blackened catfish.

**Restaurant Recipe**

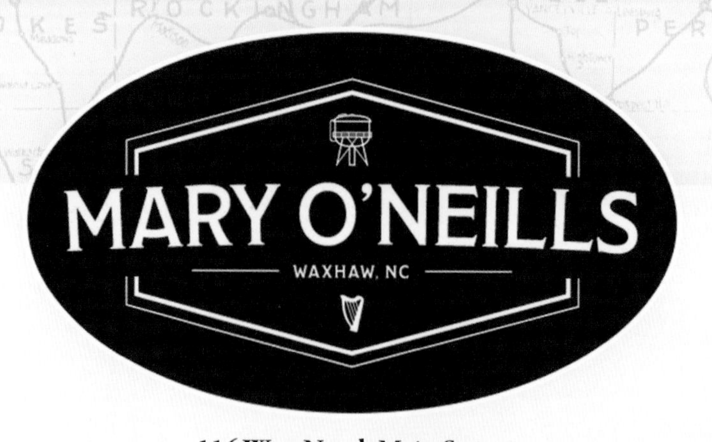


**116 West North Main Street**
**Waxhaw, NC 28173**
**704-256-7800**
**www.maryoneills.com • Find us on Facebook**

Welcome to Mary O'Neills, a friendly, welcoming pub sat right in the shadow of the Waxhaw water tower. Home of great pints and hearty cuisine, Mary O'Neills boasts an atmosphere that feels just like home, where a memory made today is a story that lasts a lifetime. Reclaimed wood and red brick hearkens back to a simpler time in which hard work was rewarded with a cold drink, good conversation, and laughter aplenty. Enjoy soups and salads, chicken wings, burgers, wraps, fish and chips, shepherd's pie, and more. Visit Mary O'Neills for Southern-inspired Irish hospitality.

**Monday – Friday: 11:00 am to 2:00 am**
**Saturday & Sunday: 10:00 am to 2:00 am**

## *Potato Leek Soup*

**32 leeks, chopped**
**½ cup minced garlic**
**1 stick butter**
**1½ cups white wine**
**22 quarts Yukon potatoes**
**12 quarts chicken stock**
**10 bay leaves**
**4 ounces fresh thyme**
**2 quarts heavy cream**
**⅓ cup black pepper**

In a large stockpot over medium-high heat, sauté leeks and garlic in butter until soft. Add wine and reduce heat to medium-low. Add potatoes, stock, bay leaves and thyme. Cook until potatoes are soft, then remove bay leaves and thyme. Add cream and pepper; blend with a hand mixer or immersion blender until smooth.

**Restaurant Recipe**

## *Water Tower Salad*

**Mixed greens**
**2 ounces craisins**
**2 ounces goat cheese**
**Slivered almonds to taste**
**Cucumber slices to taste**
**Diced tomato to taste**
**Apple vinaigrette to taste**

Toss together all ingredients in a salad bowl. Usually served with Mary O'Neills' secret, house-made apple vinaigrette, top the Water Tower Salad with your own homemade apple vinaigrette or a store-bought variety of choice.

**Restaurant Recipe**

## Downtown Deli & Café

**1 West 4th Street**
**Winston-Salem, NC 27101**
**336-721-1750**
**www.downtowndelicafe.com • Find us on Facebook**

Downtown Deli & Café opened in Downtown Winston-Salem over twenty years ago and remains the most popular restaurant on 4th Street. At Downtown Deli, you'll be treated like family from the time you walk in the door. The restaurant features over eighty menu items, including gourmet sandwiches, subs, burgers, salads, wraps, and homemade desserts. Having trouble deciding what to order? Owners Lee Charleville and Scott Nifong will be happy to suggest the perfect dish. Relax, have a good time, and eat great food when you visit Downtown Deli & Café, where having a meal is like eating with friends.

**Monday – Friday: 8:00 am to 3:00 pm**

## *Lee's Favorite*

**Button mushrooms, sliced**
**Green bell peppers, sliced**
**Red onions, sliced**
**1 (15-ounce) bottle Italian dressing**
**5 ounces smoked turkey, sliced**
**1 slice pepper Jack cheese**
**Brioche bun**

In a zip-close bag, marinate vegetables in Italian dressing overnight in the refrigerator. Next day, grill smoked turkey until heated through; add marinated vegetables and cheese over top, allowing cheese to melt. While cheese melts, slice brioche bun and toast on grill. Scoop turkey, vegetables and cheese onto bottom bun, top with top bun and serve.

Restaurant Recipe

## *Scott's Favorite*

**8 ounces Ahi-grade tuna steak**
**Cajun seasoning to taste**
**1 slice pepper Jack cheese**
**Brioche bun**
**Lettuce**
**Honey mustard dressing**

Season tuna with Cajun seasoning to taste; grill until medium-rare. Top tuna with cheese. While cheese melts, slice brioche bun and toast on grill. Scoop tuna and cheese onto bottom bun, top with lettuce and honey mustard and place top bun over top.

Restaurant Recipe

# Coastal

NORTH
CAROLINA
Cape Hatteras Lighthouse
34
USA
NORTH CAROLINA
1789
FIRST FLIGHT
2001
E PLURIBUS UNUM

GUEST CHECK
DATE
SERVER
TABLE
GUESTS
CHECK NUMBER
689561
1 Cheese burger 5 49
2 Onion Ring 4 88
1 chicken Wraps 5 99
16 36
1 15
17 51
Thank You - Please Come Again

# Mayo's Seafood Restaurant

**13533 Main Street**
**Bayboro, NC 28515**
**252-745-4663**
**Find us on Facebook**

Welcome to Mayo's Seafood Restaurant, one of Pamlico County's best-kept secret. Opened in 2012, Mayo's serves up tasty seafood, sandwiches, steaks, barbecue, burgers, wraps, and sides galore. Try appetizers like crab dip, calamari, and bacon cheddar fries. Sample tasty twists like Philly steak burgers, crab cake sandwiches, and shrimp-n-grits. You can also enjoy a barbecue plate featuring delicious, fresh Eastern Carolina barbecue. Pair your meal with a range of sides, from fried okra and steamed broccoli to homemade chips and corn nuggets. Stop by Mayo's Seafood Restaurant today.

**Monday – Thursday: 11:00 am to 8:00 pm**
**Friday & Saturday: 11:00 am to 8:30 pm**
**Sunday: 11:00 am to 2:00 pm**

## *Crab Dip*

**2 (6-ounce) cans crabmeat, drained and flaked**
**2 (8-ounce) packages cream cheese, softened**
**3 tablespoons powdered sugar**
**1½ teaspoons Worcestershire sauce**
**¼ teaspoon garlic powder**
**½ cup sour cream**
**½ teaspoon lemon juice**
**1 small red onion, chopped**
**Grated sharp Cheddar cheese for topping**

Preheat oven to 350°. In a medium bowl, mix all ingredients except cheese until well combined. Spread mixture into a 1-quart baking dish. Bake 20 minutes. Top with cheese and return to oven until melted. Pairs great with pita chips or toasted bread.

**Restaurant Recipe**

## *Shrimp-n-Grits*

**7 cups heavy cream, divided**
**1 cup uncooked instant grits**
**1 teaspoon salt, divided**
**¼ teaspoon fresh ground pepper**
**2 sticks butter, divided**
**1 large onion, chopped**
**1 each orange and yellow bell pepper, sliced**
**1 cup all-purpose flour**
**6 slices bacon, chopped and fried crisp, reserving ¼ cup grease**
**4 cloves garlic, minced**
**3 cups chicken stock**
**¼ teaspoon white pepper**
**2 pounds medium shrimp, peeled, deveined and sautéed**

In a saucepan, bring 4 cups heavy cream to a boil; stir in grits and cook, stirring occasionally, 5 to 7 minutes or until thickened. Stir in ½ teaspoon salt, pepper and ½ stick butter; set aside, keeping warm. In a large nonstick skillet over medium-high heat, cook onion and peppers 5 minutes. In a large saucepan over low heat, add flour, reserved bacon grease and garlic; brown to create a roux, then cool. Add stock, remaining heavy cream, remaining salt and white pepper; whisk sauce over low heat until thickened. Spoon grits onto individual plates; top with shrimp, peppers, onion and sauce. Garnish with bacon and serve immediately.

**Restaurant Recipe**

**1600 Haw Branch Road**
**Beulaville, NC 28518**
**910-324-3422 or 1-888-820-FARM (3276)**
**www.mikesfarm.com • Find us on Facebook**

Mike's Farm serves up family-style dishes with a touch of country. The walls are covered with antiques, photos, and trinkets of local historical significance. There are also comfortable rocking chairs on the front porch for relaxing while you wait or for recuperating in after eating till your buttons pop. Take a seat at one of the large farm tables and dig in as you are served bowls of fried chicken with all the fixin's. The menu features the best of down-home country cooking, including fried chicken, country ham biscuits, mashed potatoes, macaroni and cheese, and corn. You can even top it off with a sweet dessert. At Mike's Farm, you'll never leave hungry!

**Call for Hours of Operation**

## *Gingersnap Cookies*

**2 cups sugar plus more for rolling**
**1½ cups oil**
**2 eggs**
**½ cup molasses**
**4 cups all-purpose flour**
**4 teaspoons baking soda**
**3 teaspoons ginger**
**2 teaspoons cinnamon**
**1 teaspoon salt**
**Melted white chocolate for topping**

Preheat oven to 350°. In a bowl, combine sugar and oil. Beat in eggs, then stir in molasses. In another bowl, combine flour, baking soda, ginger, cinnamon and salt; gradually stir into wet mixture until combined. Sprinkle a plate with sugar. Shape dough into ¾-inch balls; roll in sugar on plate. Arrange on a baking sheet, 2 inches apart. Bake 10 to 12 minutes; cool, then drizzle cookies with white chocolate.

**Bakery Recipe**

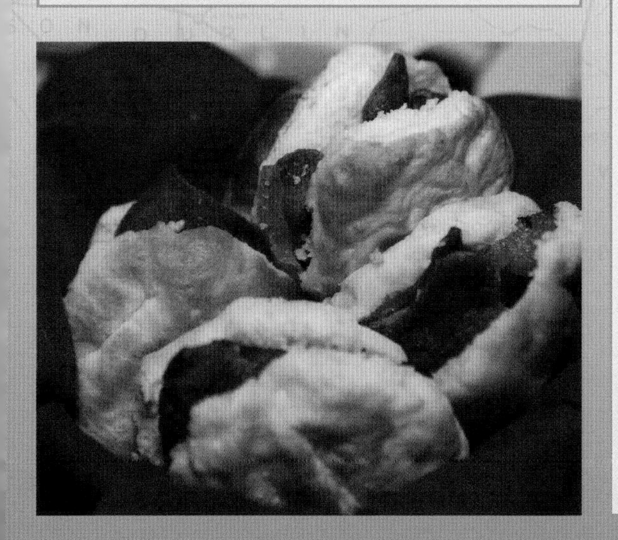

## *Pumpkin Praline Cake*

**Flour for dusting**
**1 box yellow cake mix**
**1 cup pumpkin purée**
**1 cup whole milk**
**¼ cup vegetable oil**
**4 large eggs**
**½ cup chopped pecans**
**½ teaspoon nutmeg**
**¾ teaspoon cinnamon**

Preheat oven to 350°. Grease two 8-inch, round cake pans with nonstick spray and dust with flour. In a bowl, mix remaining ingredients until moistened, being sure to scrape down sides; divide batter evenly between prepared pans. Bake 27 minutes; cake is done when a toothpick inserted into center comes out clean. Remove from oven and cool.

### *Pecan Glaze:*

**2 (14-ounce) cans sweetened condensed milk**
**4 tablespoons unsalted butter**
**1 cup chopped pecans**

In a saucepan over medium heat, combine all ingredients. Stir, heating just until butter melts; set aside. Invert a cake layer onto a plate, poke holes with a wooden spoon and pour a third Glaze over layer. Invert second layer over top of first, pokes holes again and pour another third Glaze over top. Cool remaining icing until slightly thickened, then pour over top of cake.

**Family Favorite**

# North Banks Restaurant & Raw Bar

**794 Sunset Boulevard, #G**
**Corolla, NC 27927**
**252-453-3344**
**www.northbanks.com • Find us on Facebook**

North Banks Restaurant & Raw Bar has been a seafood establishment favorite of Corolla locals for over 20 years. Daily lunch and dinner specials feature fresh, local fish and creative sauces. The raw bar boasts steamed North Carolina shrimp, Maine lobster, littleneck clams, regional and select oysters, and snow crab legs. North Banks takes pride in preparing all its sauces and dressings, hand cutting its croutons, and filleting all its fresh fish. A local butcher blends and grinds its burgers and hand cuts its filet mignon and other beef items. At North Banks, only the freshest produce and ingredients available are used. Come experience the freshest seafood in Corolla.

**Lunch & Dinner:**
**Daily: 11:30 am until**

## *Asian Slaw*

**4 quarts dressed coleslaw**
**¾ cup teriyaki sauce**
**¼ cup sesame oil**
**6 tablespoons black and white sesame seeds**

In a large mixing bowl, combine all ingredients until thoroughly incorporated. Enjoy.

**Restaurant Recipe**

## *Poblano-Pecan Mustard Butter*

**½ cup pecans**
**2 pounds butter, softened**
**⅓ cup whole-grain mustard**
**¼ cup rough-chopped red onion**
**1 teaspoon freshly minced garlic**
**2 poblano peppers, roasted, peeled, seeded and chopped**

In a food processor, combine all ingredients. Blend until smooth. Enjoy.

**Restaurant Recipe**

# Cape Fear Winery

**195 Vineyard Drive**
**Elizabethtown, NC 28337**
**844-846-3386**
**www.capefearwinery.com**
**Find us on Facebook**

The Cork Room at Cape Fear Vineyard & Winery offers a unique dining experience, featuring an eclectic and acclaimed menu. Each wine in The Cork Room's collection is produced to linger on the palate, accenting the flavors of the cuisine served. Southern beef, poultry, pork, seafood, and harvest vegetables all pair perfectly with the selection of available house and estate wines. The creative team of chefs at The Cork Room strive, often as possible, to include local, farm-to-table vegetables, meats, and seafood choices in their dishes. Locally sourced ingredients guarantee guests the freshest, tastiest dining experience available, every time. Relax and get away from it all with The Cork Room.

The Cork Room

**Wednesday: 11:30 am to 9:00 pm**
**Thursday – Saturday: 11:30 am to 10:00 pm**
**Sunday: 11:30 am to 3:00 pm**

## *Pimento Cheese*

**4 cups shredded Cheddar cheese**
**4 (8-ounce) packages cream cheese, softened**
**8 cups mayonnaise**
**1 teaspoon granulated garlic**
**1 small pinch ghost pepper flakes**
**1 teaspoon onion powder**
**1 teaspoon black pepper**
**1 teaspoon salt**
**2 cups diced roasted red peppers**

Combine all ingredients in the bowl of a stand mixer. Beat on medium speed until well combined.

Restaurant Recipe

## *She-Crab Soup*

**8 ounces butter**
**16 ounces flour**
**½ cup olive oil**
**4 cups mirepoix**
**1 tablespoons puréed garlic**
**1 cup white wine**
**1 (8-ounce) can clam juice**
**½ cup honey**
**1 gallon chicken stock**
**1 cup sherry**
**2 onions, diced**
**1 head celery, diced**
**1 pound carrots, diced**
**1 teaspoon white pepper**
**Pinch ground cloves**
**2 tablespoons paprika**
**Pinch nutmeg**
**½ teaspoon cayenne**
**3 tablespoons ground mustard**
**6 bay leaves**
**1 tablespoon tobacco**
**1 tablespoon chopped fresh thyme**
**2 teaspoons dill**
**2 quarts heavy cream**
**1 quart half-and-half**
**3 (6-ounce) cans crabmeat**
**Salt to taste**

In a saucepan over medium heat, melt butter; stir in flour and oil to wet-sand consistency. Not all flour may be needed. Cook over low heat until roux is lightly browned. In a large stockpot, sauté mirepoix and garlic 5 minutes over medium-high heat; deglaze with wine, reducing until almost dry. Add clam juice, honey, stock, sherry, vegetables, spices, herbs and heavy cream; reduce heat to low and bring to a simmer. Vigorously whisk in prepared roux and bring back to a simmer. Thin soup with half-and-half and gently stir in crab. Season with salt to taste.

Restaurant Recipe

# The Scullery

**431 Evans Street**
**Greenville, NC 27858**
**252-321-1550**
**Find us on Facebook**

Welcome to The Scullery, home of fresh roasted coffee, homemade ice creams, and delicious food prepared with fresh, locally sourced ingredients. This quaint eatery serves breakfast, lunch and everything in between. Settle down to a bowl of some the best grits you'll ever taste, or take your pick of other menu items, from soups and salads to sandwiches and desserts. The Scullery also specializes in gourmet coffee creations, like the caramello, a latte made with caramel sauce, or the vanilla bee, a latte made with vanilla and local honey. Whatever you decide to order, you won't be disappointed, as The Scullery has something to suit every taste.

**Monday – Friday: 7:00 am to 5:00 pm**
**Saturday: 8:00 am to 5:00 pm**

## *Bacon Scramble*

**1 teaspoon butter**
**6 slices bacon, chopped into ¼-inch pieces**
**6 eggs**
**Salt and pepper to taste**
**¼ cup shredded Cheddar cheese**

In a skillet over medium-high heat, add butter; fry bacon pieces until crisp. Meanwhile, whisk eggs with salt and pepper in another bowl until incorporated. Spread bacon around skillet, then add egg mixture. Using a spatula, gently fold bacon into the eggs as they cook. When done, remove from heat and sprinkle with Cheddar. Serves 3 and pairs great with a hot coffee and jam-smeared toast.

**Restaurant Recipe**

## *BLAT Sandwich*

**1 cup mayonnaise**
**1 cup softened cream cheese**
**¼ cup dried basil**
**Salt and pepper to taste**
**2 slices multi-grain bread, toasted**
**4 strips bacon, cooked crisp**
**½ cup chopped lettuce**
**½ avocado, sliced**
**2 slices tomato**

In a bowl, add mayonnaise, cream cheese, basil, salt and pepper; beat with a hand mixer until fully combined. To assemble sandwich, place 1 slice toasted bread down and smear with mayonnaise mixture. Top with bacon, lettuce and avocado. Season tomatoes with salt and pepper and add to sandwich. Finish by topping with remaining slice toasted bread, cut in half and enjoy with a cold beer or a glass of fresh lemonade.

**Restaurant Recipe**

# Captain Bob's Barbeque & Seafood

**310 Ocean Highway South**
**Hertford, NC 27944**
**252-426-1811**
**www.captainbobs.net • Find us on Facebook**

To find good, home-style country cooking, look no further than Captain Bob's Barbeque & Seafood. Enjoy pit-smoked barbecue cooked on site. In addition to delicious barbecue, Captain Bob's also offers fresh seafood. Owner Bobby Lane is a longtime local commercial fisherman who decided to venture into the restaurant business some 19 years ago. When he's not on the water, Bobby's helping run the restaurant with wife, Sharon. It should come as no surprise that guests can find delights like grilled or blackened tuna steaks, homemade crab cakes, pickled herring, whole flounder, and more. With a friendly staff of nearly 40 employees, Captain Bob's will keep you coming back for more.

**Monday – Friday: 7:00 am to 8:30 pm**
**Saturday: 7:00 am to 9:00 pm**
**Sunday: 8:00 am to 8:30 pm**

## *Brunswick Stew*

**1 tablespoon chicken base**
**1 cup hot sauce**
**1 chicken, cooked, deboned and diced**
**4 cups chopped cabbage**
**2 potatoes, diced**
**2 (15.25-ounce) cans lima beans**
**2 (15-ounce) cans sweet peas**
**2 cups ketchup**
**2 (15.25-ounce) cans whole-kernel corn**
**2 cups chopped tomato**

In a large stockpot, add chicken base, hot sauce, chicken, cabbage, potatoes and water to cover; bring to a boil, then reduce heat to a simmer. Cook 15 minutes or until potatoes are fork-tender and cabbage is translucent. Stir in remaining ingredients and cook until heated through. Enjoy.

**Restaurant Recipe**

## *Crab Salad*

**½ cup chopped green onion**
**3 green bell peppers, diced**
**3 stalks celery, diced**
**¼ cup mayonnaise**
**8 cups ranch dressing**
**2 pounds crabmeat, chopped**
**Old Bay seasoning to taste**

In a large bowl, stir together vegetables, mayonnaise and ranch. Fold in crabmeat, taking care not to break up. Fold in Old Bay to taste.

**Restaurant Recipe**

**1216 South Virginia Dare Trail**
**Kill Devil Hills, NC 27948**
**252-441-7994**
**www.fooddudeskitchenobx.com • Find us on Facebook**

Food Dudes Kitchen boasts a varied menu of Caribbean-inspired dishes, each featuring a little Mexican flare yet remaining true to the Outer Banks' culinary roots and classic Southern fare. Sample appetizers, like chili garlic shrimp spring rolls and pico de gallo; tasty entrees, like sweet-chili-glazed fish and pan-sautéed crab cakes; and inventive quesadillas and wraps, like barbecue chicken quesadillas and jerk chicken wraps. Food Dudes also offers a variety of sandwiches and burgers as well as a rotating daily dessert special. Drop 'n' dine at mile post 9 for Outer Banks seafood at its finest.

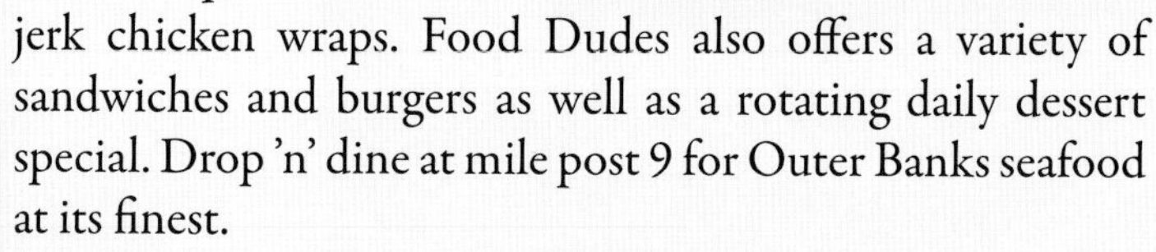

**Daily: 11:30 am to 9:00 pm**

## *Sweet-Chili-Glazed Mahi-Mahi*

**½ cup chopped pineapple**
**¼ cup chopped mango**
**1 bunch cilantro, finely chopped**
**¼ cup chopped red onion**
**¼ cup chopped roasted red pepper**
**⅛ cup chopped roasted poblano pepper**
**1 lime, juiced**
**1 cup cooked jasmine rice**
**1 fillet mahi-mahi, grilled or blackened**
**Mae Ploy sweet chili sauce to taste**

To make pineapple-mango salsa: add pineapple, mango, cilantro, onion, red pepper, poblano pepper and lime juice to a bowl; fold together to combine. On a plate, spread rice to make a bed, then top with pineapple-mango salsa. Top with mahi-mahi; glaze with sweet chili sauce. Enjoy.

**Restaurant Recipe**

# Barrier Island Bagels

**5549 North Croatan Highway**
**Kitty Hawk, NC 27949**
**252-255-2888**
**www.barrierislandbagels.com • Find us on Facebook**

Located at the Marketplace Shopping Center in Southern Shores, Barrier Island Bagels is a convenient stop for a delicious breakfast or lunch. At Barrier Island Bagels, they settle for nothing less than the best. Never frozen and made with the best ingredients on the market, their handmade bagels are prepared daily to ensure the freshest, most delicious bagels on the Outer Banks. The shop also offers açaí bowls and seven house-special customizable smoothies. The delectable deli features subs and sandwiches made with quality Boar's Head meats. Don't forget to try the homemade chicken salad. Come see why Barrier Island Bagels is the best of the beach.

**Daily: 7:00 am to 2:00 pm**

# *Chicken Crescent Squares*

**4 boneless chicken breasts**
**1 large Vidalia onion**
**1 (8-ounce) package cream cheese, softened**
**Salt and pepper to taste**
**2 (8-ounce) packages Pillsbury dough sheets**
**Melted butter**
**Italian breadcrumbs for topping**

Preheat oven to 350°. In a saucepan, add chicken and water to cover. Boil chicken until done; cool and shred. In a food processor, finely mince onion. In a large mixing bowl, stir together chicken, onion, cream cheese, salt and pepper. On a nonstick-sprayed surface, lay out dough sheets and cut evenly into 16 squares. Place a spoonful of chicken mixture on 8 squares and top each with a remaining square. Transfer to a 9-inch square baking dish. Brush with butter and top with breadcrumbs. Bake 30 minutes or until golden brown.

**Restaurant Recipe**

# Capt'n Franks

**3800 North Croatan Highway**
**Kitty Hawk, NC 27949**
**252-261-9923**
**www.captnfranks.com • Find us on Facebook**

In 1975, back when the bypass was still two-laned, the Hess family opened a summer hot dog shop—Capt'n Franks. Capt'n Franks is one of a disappearing breed that once populated Atlantic beaches from Rehoboth to Fort Lauderdale. What the drive-in diner was to city kids, small hot dog stands and walk-up burger joints with fresh, crispy French fries were to the beach experience. Sand-swept floors, bathing-suit-clad patrons, and maybe the owner's dog napping under an empty table were all common features of beach-front restaurants. For an experience that is second to none, visit Capt'n Franks and decide for yourself whether they serve the best hot dog in the world.

**Monday – Saturday: 10:30 am to 3:00 pm**

## *World-Famous Steamed Shrimp with Cocktail Sauce*

### *Cocktail Sauce:*

**½ cup ketchup**
**1 heaping tablespoon ground horseradish**
**1 tablespoon lemon juice**

In a bowl, mix all ingredients until smooth. Chill while cooking shrimp.

### *Shrimp:*

**1 pint white vinegar**
**½ cup Old Bay seasoning**
**2 to 3 tablespoons lemon juice, optional**
**1 pound (36/40-size) unpeeled shrimp**
**Old Bay or Creole seasoning for sprinkling, optional**
**Melted butter, optional**
**Lemon slices, optional**

In a large stockpot, bring 2 quarts water plus white vinegar to a slow rolling boil. Add Old Bay seasoning; boil until seasoning absorbs. If desired, add 2 to 3 tablespoons lemon juice. Stir shrimp into boiling mixture, cooking about 1½ minutes; remove from pot with a colander and set aside. For mild shrimp, you are done. For Outer Banks-style shrimp, sprinkle and toss with additional Old Bay seasoning. For Louisiana-style shrimp, sprinkle and toss with Creole seasoning. Cool and serve with Cocktail Sauce, melted butter and fresh lemon slices.

Restaurant Recipe

# *The* BANKS GRILL

**2900 Arendell Street**
**Morehead City, NC 28557**
**252-499-9044**
**www.thebanksgrill.com • Find us on Facebook**

Welcome to The Banks Grill, the best place on the Crystal Coast to get a delicious made-to-order breakfast and lunch. Come in and relax as you spread homemade jelly on your extra-extra-large fresh-baked biscuit, or savor a great cup of coffee as you await a plate of scratch-made biscuits and gravy made with hand-mixed sausage. At lunch, revel in the beachy atmosphere while dining on the incredible tuna salad made with locally caught bounty. The Banks Grill's outstanding food, service, and atmosphere will keep you coming back over and over again.

**Monday & Wednesday – Friday:**
**7:00 am to 2:00 pm**
**Saturday & Sunday: 7:30 am to 2:00 pm**

## *Blueberry-Nut Bread*

**2 cups sifted flour**
**3 teaspoons baking powder**
**¼ teaspoon salt**
**1 cup sugar**
**1 cup blueberries**
**½ cup chopped nuts**
**2 eggs, well beaten**
**1 cup milk**
**3 tablespoons melted shortening or vegetable oil**

Sift dry ingredients into a large bowl. Stir in blueberries and nuts. In another bowl, whisk together eggs, milk and shortening; add to dry ingredients and stir in slightly. Pour into a parchment-lined loaf pan; let sit 30 minutes. Bake at 350° for 1 hour.

Local Favorite

## *Broiled Chicken*

**6 skinless chicken breasts**
**1 stick margarine, cubed and divided**
**Worcestershire sauce**
**⅓ cup apple cider vinegar**
**1 teaspoon salt**
**2 bay leaves**

Preheat oven to 350°. Dot each breast with margarine. Coat with Worcestershire sauce. Place chicken in small, lidded roasting pan with vinegar, salt, bay leaves and enough water to almost cover. Bake 1 hour. Remove top of pan, dot with butter again and broil until golden brown. Remove bay leaves and thicken gravy slightly.

Local Favorite

# BLUE MOON BEACH GRILL

Milepost 13, Surfside Plaza Nags Head, NC

**4104 South Virginia Dare Trail**
**Nags Head, NC 27959**
**252-261-BLUE (2583)**
**www.bluemoonbeachgrill.com • Follow us on Facebook and Instagram**

Welcome to Blue Moon Beach Grill, where you are sure to experience a quirky, fun-filled dining experience. Though it may be small, Blue Moon Beach Grill makes up for its size with big personality. Guests will enjoy Southern comfort food with an added creative twist and flair. For those on a tight budget, the Grill always tries to maintain affordable prices. Try out the daily specials, and be sure to watch the blackboard for some amazingly inventive specials. Come out to Blue Moon Beach Grill for cordial service, tasty food, and, of course, a "once in a blue moon" experience.

**Daily: 11:30 am to 9:00 pm**

## *Spicy Feta Dip*

**8 ounces goat cheese**
**1 roasted red bell pepper, seeded and diced**
**1 jalapeño pepper, seeded and finely chopped**
**¼ cup extra virgin olive oil plus more for topping**
**½ tablespoon hot smoked paprika plus more for topping**
**6 ounces feta cheese, crumbled**
**2 tablespoons fresh chopped parsley plus more for topping**
**3 tablespoons fresh chopped dill plus more for topping**
**Sea salt and fresh ground black pepper**

In a food processor, combine goat cheese, bell pepper, jalapeño, oil and paprika; blend until smooth. Transfer mixture to a medium mixing bowl; stir in feta, parsley, dill, sea salt and pepper. Transfer to a serving bowl; top with additional oil, herbs and a sprinkle of paprika.

**Chef Nathan Robinson**

## *Blue Moon Crab Cakes*

**1 tablespoon mayonnaise**
**1 egg**
**½ teaspoon prepared mustard**
**½ teaspoon Old Bay seasoning**
**2 dashes Tabasco sauce**
**¼ teaspoon celery salt**
**1 tablespoon chopped parsley**
**2 tablespoons Japanese breadcrumbs**
**2 tablespoons Autry Seafood Breading**
**1 pound lump crabmeat**
**Oil for frying**

In a bowl, combine mayonnaise, egg, mustard, Old Bay, Tabasco, celery salt and parsley; whisk together until smooth. In a separate bowl, combine breadcrumbs and seafood breading. Fold crabmeat into wet ingredients. Slowly fold breadings into crab mixture; set aside 30 minutes. Portion mixture into crab cakes of desired size. To cook, pan fry in oil 4 to 5 minutes each side or deep fry 4 to 5 minutes until crisp and browned. Serve with Blue Moon Jalapeño Remoulade Sauce.

**Restaurant Recipe**

## *Blue Moon Jalapeño Remoulade Sauce*

*This signature remoulade has been a customer favorite since Blue Moon opened. It's served with the Mahi BLT, crab cakes and fish & chips.*

**1 gallon mayonnaise**
**4 ribs celery, finely diced**
**1 cup finely chopped green onions**
**12 jalapeño peppers, grilled, seeded and minced**
**2 cups horseradish**
**1 cup Gulden's mustard**
**½ cup yellow mustard**
**2 tablespoons smoked paprika**
**2 tablespoons black pepper**
**1½ cups dried parsley**
**3 tablespoons minced garlic**
**¼ cup Frank's hot sauce**

In a large mixing bowl, add all ingredients. Mix until well-combined. Refrigerate until ready to serve. Makes 6 quarts.

**Restaurant Recipe**

# Mulligan's Grille

**4005 South Croatan Highway**
**Nags Head, NC 27959**
**252-480-2000**
**www.mulligansobx.com**
**Find us on Facebook**

Known for serving the "Best Burger on the Beach" for over 20 years, Mulligan's Grille is quickly earning a reputation for the best local seafood as well. In keeping with traditional Southern coastal cuisine and the farm-to-fork philosophy, Mulligan's green-tail shrimp and oysters come right from the waters of the Pamlico Sound, while the produce used is grown on farms in Currituck County. Mulligan's recycles their vegetable frying oil, cardboard delivery boxes, oyster shells, and glass bottles. In addition to biodegradable carryout bags, the restaurant also uses recycled paper products for carryout containers and napkins. Visit today for local, sustainable seafood fished right from North Carolina waters.

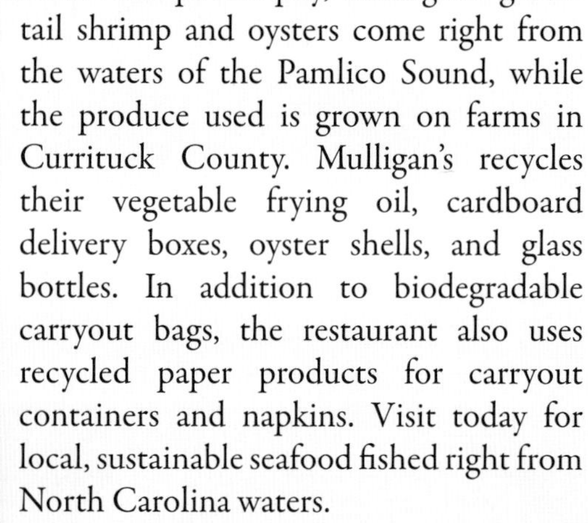

**Monday – Friday: 11:00 am to midnight**
**Saturday & Sunday: 10:00 am to midnight**

## *Shrimp & Grits Poppers*

**4 poblano peppers**
**3½ cups cooked grits**
**1 cup shredded Cheddar cheese**
**2 tablespoons Cajun seasoning**
**16 jumbo shrimp, grilled**
**Pico de gallo for garnish**
**Chipotle aioli for garnish**

Preheat oven to 350°. When heated, roast poblanos 4 minutes; cool, then cut a slit lengthwise. Scoop out seeds and discard. In a bowl, mix remaining ingredients except shrimp; stuff poblanos with mixture, then top each with 4 interlocking shrimp. Return to oven, baking 8 to 10 minutes or just until heated through. Garnish with pico de gallo and drizzle with chipotle aioli before serving.

Restaurant Recipe

## *Coconut Shrimp*

**2 dozen jumbo shrimp**
**1 cup seafood breader**
**Shaved coconut for coating**

In a bowl, mix seafood breader with ¾ cup water, adjusting mixture to consistency of pancake batter by adding more breader or water if needed. Peel, devein and wash shrimp; pat dry with a paper towel, then lay out on cutting board. Butterfly shrimp by cutting down the back and spreading apart. Spread out shaved coconut on a plate, dip shrimp into breader to coat and roll in shaved coconut, coating well. Line tray with prepared shrimp; refrigerate 2 hours. Preheat deep fryer to 350°; fry shrimp until golden brown. Serve with your favorite sauce.

Restaurant Recipe

# Toucan Grill & Fresh Bar

**103 Wall Street**
**Oriental, NC 28571**
**252-249-2204**
**www.toucangrill.com • Find us on Facebook**

Inside the Toucan Grill & Fresh Bar, you will find a bright and festive atmosphere that is home to great food and colorful characters. The Toucan Crew invites you to come in and enjoy a relaxing meal. Dine on everything from burgers and sandwiches to soups and salads as well as a range of specialty entrees. While eating, you can watch shrimp trawlers "pack out" fresh seafood, carrying on a proud North Carolina tradition. On weekends, head over to the Tiki Bar patio for live music and entertainment.

Lunch:
**Friday – Sunday:**
**Noon to 5:00 pm**
Dinner:
**Monday & Wednesday – Sunday:**
**5:00 pm to 9:00 pm**

## *Shrimp & Scallop Carbonara*

**1 pound thick-cut Applewood-smoked bacon, large-diced**

**2 medium yellow onions, thinly sliced**

**2 tablespoons minced garlic**

**1 pound (26/30) shrimp, peeled, deveined and washed**

**1 pound medium scallops, heels removed**

**1 quart heavy cream**

**3 cups shredded Parmesan cheese plus more for topping**

**Kosher salt and coarse ground black pepper to taste**

**1 pound linguini pasta, cooked al dente and cooled**

In a large saucepan over medium heat, slowly render bacon until it begins to crisp. Add onion and garlic, cooking until onion is translucent. Add shrimp and scallops, stirring with bacon and vegetables until half-cooked, about 2 minutes. Add heavy cream, then reduce by half. Remove pan from heat and stir in Parmesan until melted. Add salt and pepper to taste. Toss cooked pasta with sauce and plate on serving dishes. Finish each dish with a sprinkle of Parmesan.

Restaurant Recipe

## *Toucan Original Crab Dip*

**1½ (8-ounce) packages cream cheese, softened**

**¼ tablespoon crushed beef bouillon**

**1 (8-ounce) container sour cream**

**4 cups shredded Parmesan cheese plus more for topping**

**2 ounces seeded and minced jalapeño peppers**

**1¼ pounds crabmeat (lump, jumbo lump or back fin)**

**Toasted pita or crackers for serving**

Preheat oven to 400°. In a bowl, add all ingredients except crabmeat; mix until fully combined. Fold in crabmeat, taking care not to break lumps. Transfer to an oven-safe baking dish; bake until dip begins to bubble, then sprinkle top with additional Parmesan. Broil until golden brown. Serve with toasted pita or crackers.

Restaurant Recipe

## Fishy Fishy Café

**106 Yacht Basin**
**Southport, NC 28461**
**910-457-1881**
**www.fishyfishycafe.com**
**Find us on Facebook**

Welcome to Fishy Fishy Café. Inspired by waterfront living, Fishy Fishy Café's food, casual atmosphere, and Carolina hospitality make the restaurant a Southport favorite for locals and visitors alike. Enjoy fresh seafood, fried or grilled to your taste; black Angus burgers; fresh salads; refreshing drinks from two full-service bars; live music; and world-class sunsets. Located beside the meeting point of the Cape Fear River and the Intracoastal Waterway, with views of the Yacht Basin, the marsh, and Oak Island, Fishy Fishy Café offers indoor or outdoor seating with a beautiful view year-round. Relax at Fishy Fishy Café and let the attentive staff take care of the rest.

**Monday – Thursday: 11:00 am to 8:00 pm**
**Friday & Saturday: 11:00 am to 9:00 pm**
**Sunday: 11:00 am to 8:00 pm**

## *Fishy's Bloody Mary Mix*

**1 (46-ounce) can V8 juice**
**1 teaspoon black pepper**
**2 tablespoons A.1. steak sauce**
**1 teaspoon Tabasco sauce**
**2 tablespoons celery salt**
**2 tablespoons horseradish**
**2 tablespoons Worcestershire sauce**
**2 tablespoons lime juice**
**6 ounces vodka**
**Celery stalks, green olives, lemon slices, lime slices and chilled cocktail shrimp for garnish**

In a pitcher, combine all ingredients except vodka; refrigerate before serving. Stir in vodka just before serving. Pour into a glass, then garnish with 1 stalk celery, 2 olives, a lemon slice, a lime slice and a cocktail shrimp. Enjoy. Makes about 4 drinks.

**Restaurant Recipe**

## *Fishy's Cobb Salad with Balsamic Dressing*

### *Cobb Salad:*

**3 cups mixed greens**
**¼ cup blue cheese crumbles**
**¼ cup halved cherry tomatoes**
**¼ cup cooked and chopped bacon**
**1 egg, hard-boiled and sliced**
**1 chicken breast, grilled and chopped**

In a bowl, add mixed greens. Add blue cheese, cherry tomatoes and bacon. Arrange sliced egg around edges. Top salad with chicken.

### *Balsamic Dressing:*

**1 cup balsamic vinegar**
**¼ cup white vinegar**
**2 tablespoons Dijon mustard**
**1 teaspoon honey**
**Pinch each salt and pepper**
**Pinch Italian seasoning**
**1 teaspoon garlic**
**2 cups olive oil**

Mix all ingredients except olive oil in a bowl until smooth; slowly whisk in olive oil a little at a time. Chill, then pour over salad before serving.

**Restaurant Recipe**

# Provision Company

**130 Yacht Basin Drive**
**Southport, NC 28461**
**910-457-0654**
**www.provisioncompany.com • Find us on Facebook**

Provision Company, called "Provisions" by locals, was established in 1993 and serves some of the best food in town. After dining, take a short walk to see the most beautiful scenery in the beloved, sunny little town of Southport. Views of the Southport Yacht Basin, the Intracoastal Waterway, and the mouth of the Cape Fear River are incredible, and the sunsets, magnificent. A short drive will place you at over thirteen miles of Oak Island beaches, while a four-mile ferry ride will take you to one of the most unique islands in the Carolinas, Bald Head Island. Stop by Provision Company for great seafood in a casual, waterfront atmosphere.

**Daily: 11:00 am to 9:00 pm**
**March 17th into November**

## *Conch Fritters*

**1 quart vegetable oil**
**½ cup milk**
**¾ cup flour**
**1 egg**
**1 cup chopped conch**
**2 cloves garlic, chopped**
**½ onion, chopped**
**1 stalk celery, chopped**
**½ red bell pepper, chopped**
**3 tablespoons freshly chopped parsley**
**Salt and pepper to taste**
**Dash Tabasco sauce**

In a large stockpot, preheat oil to 365°. In a large bowl, mix milk, flour and egg until smooth. Stir in remaining ingredients until combined. Drop batter by the tablespoonful into hot oil; fry until golden brown and drain on a paper towel. Serve with Remoulade Sauce.

Restaurant Recipe

## *Remoulade Sauce*

**¾ cup mayonnaise**
**2 tablespoons chopped onion**
**1 tablespoon stone-ground mustard**
**1 tablespoon ketchup**
**1 teaspoon horseradish**
**Pinch garlic**
**Salt and pepper to taste**
**Tabasco sauce to taste**

In a food processor, combine all ingredients. Blend and refrigerate before serving. Pairs great with Conch Fritters.

Restaurant Recipe

# The Country Squire Restaurant, Inn & Winery

**748 North Carolina Highway 24B/50**
**Warsaw, NC 28398**
**910-296-1727**
**www.countrysquirewinery.com • Find us on Facebook**

At Country Squire Restaurant, Inn & Winery, memories are just waiting to be made. The old-world ambiance of The Country Squire has charmed guests since 1961. A pleasing atmosphere and relaxed dining in combination with free tastings at the Tartan Tasting Room & Gift Shop make this a great destination. The Country Squire also hosts special events, from romantic dinners, vineyard weddings, and family reunions to business events and club meetings. Guests may also enjoy lodging at The Squire's Vintage Inn and Guest House.

Lunch:
**Tuesday – Friday & Sunday:**
**11:30 am to 2:00 pm**
Dinner:
**Tuesday – Saturday: 5:00 pm until**
Wine-Tasting & Gift Shop:
**Tuesday – Friday: Noon to 7:00 pm**
**Saturday: Noon to 9:00 pm**

## *Pride of Scotland Five-Pepper Jelly Glaze*

*This glaze is a little spicy and great over grilled or baked chicken, pork or mild fish.*

**½ cup The Country Squire's Pride of Scotland chardonnay**
**½ cup The Country Squire's Five-Pepper Jelly**
**1 tablespoon butter**

In a saucepan over medium-high heat, add all ingredients and ¼ cup water; simmer, whisking occasionally, 5 to 10 minutes or until bubbly and smooth. Remove from heat and cool. Spoon or brush over your favorite grilled meat, or for baked meat, brush on glaze 5 to 10 minutes before removing from oven. Enjoy.

**Family Favorite**

## *The Squire's Coffee*

*A favorite cool weather treat.*

**1 ounce Frangelico liqueur**
**1 ounce Bailey's Irish Cream liqueur**
**6 ounces freshly brewed regular or decaf coffee**
**Fresh whipped cream**
**Shaved dark chocolate or dark chocolate sprinkles**

Mix liqueurs and coffee in a large mug. Top with fresh whipped cream and garnish with chocolate. For a stronger drink, you may add a little Irish whiskey.

**Restaurant Recipe**

# The Chef & the Frog

**605 South Madison Street**
**Whiteville, NC 28472**
**910-640-5550**
**www.chefnc.com • Find us on Facebook & Instagram**

Once upon a time, while living in Paris, a Cambodian princess met a frog, or so the story goes. Chef Sokun was born in Cambodia but fled persecution with her family at the age of 7. A transplant to France, she developed a talent for fusing European cuisine with Cambodian spices. She later met her French frog, Guillaume, and with nothing in their pockets and a dream in their hearts, the pair moved to America in 1998 to open a restaurant. To date, Sokun has opened three restaurants, including The Chef and the Frog, a casual fine-dining European restaurant that blends French cooking with an Asian twist and Southern flair.

Lunch:
**Tuesday – Friday: 11:00 am to 2:00 pm**
Dinner:
**Thursday – Saturday: 5:00 pm to 9:00 pm**
Brunch:
**Sunday: 11:30 am to 1:30 pm**

## *Curry Paste*

**3 stalks lemongrass, thinly sliced (only use bottom 3 inches of stalk)**

**4 makrut lime leaves, thinly slices after center rib removed**

**1 ounce galangal or ginger, peeled and finely chopped**

**8 cloves garlic, finely chopped**

**2 shallots, finely chopped**

**1 ounce turmeric, peeled and finely chopped**

With a mortar and pestle, grind lemongrass, makrut and galangal. Grind in remaining ingredients, one at a time, until combined into a paste. Refrigerate in a screw-top jar between uses.

**Restaurant Recipe**

## *Cambodian Beef*

**1 tablespoon vegetable oil**

**1 red onion, sliced**

**1 red bell pepper, sliced**

**1 green bell pepper, sliced**

**5 tablespoons prepared Curry Paste**

**Fish sauce to taste**

**Soy sauce to taste**

**Salt and pepper to taste**

**1 pound beef, sliced**

**1 cup cooked jasmine rice**

In a large skillet, heat vegetable oil; sauté vegetables until onions are translucent. Add Curry Paste, fish sauce, soy sauce, salt and pepper. Add beef and cook to medium rare or desired doneness. Serve over top of a bed of jasmine rice. Enjoy.

**Restaurant Recipe**

## *Garlic Aioli*

**2 large eggs, separated and whites discarded**
**¼ cup lemon juice**
**1 teaspoon kosher salt**
**1 teaspoon ground black pepper**
**2 tablespoons minced garlic**
**2 cups olive oil**

In a food processor, combine all ingredients except olive oil. Blend on low setting while slowly adding oil until mixture is thick like mayonnaise. Pairs great with fried green tomatoes. Keep refrigerated.

**Restaurant Recipe**

# Bill's Front Porch

**4238 Market Street**
**Wilmington, NC 28403**
**910-762-6333**
**www.billsfrontporch.com • Find us on Facebook**

Welcome to Bill's Front Porch, a pub and brewery where you'll discover fine handcrafted beers, creative yet informal cuisine, and friendly, attentive service in a casual, upscale atmosphere. Bill's is passionate about serving full-flavored, handcrafted beers and scratch-made New American cuisine in a comfortable atmosphere. The goal has always been to provide beer and food that is inspired, consistently crafted, and presented by a knowledgeable and courteous service staff. Bill's Front Porch's commitment to support the communities in which it does business goes to the heart of what differentiates Bill's from other restaurants. Come join 'em on the front porch!

**Tuesday – Thursday: 4:00 pm to 10:00 pm**
**Friday & Saturday: 11:00 am to 11:00 pm**
**Sunday: 11:00 am to 9:00 pm**

## *Fried Green Tomatoes*

**2 cups all-purpose flour**
**2 cups panko breadcrumbs**
**1 tablespoon thyme**
**1 tablespoon oregano**
**1 tablespoon kosher salt**
**1 teaspoon ground black pepper**
**1 teaspoon nutmeg**
**1 teaspoon ground coriander**
**4 large green tomatoes**
**1½ cups buttermilk**

Preheat deep fryer to 350°. In a bowl, mix dry ingredients. Slice tomatoes in ⅜-inch-thick slices, discarding tops and bottoms. Dredge tomato in dry ingredients, dip into buttermilk and dredge again in dry ingredients. Fry until golden and drain on paper towels. Serve with Purple Onion Marmalade and Garlic Aioli.

Restaurant Recipe

## *Purple Onion Marmalade*

**8 cups ¼-inch-diced red onion**
**1 cup white wine**
**1 cup red wine vinegar**
**1 cup white sugar**
**1 tablespoon kosher salt**

Combine all ingredients in a medium stockpot; bring to boil. Cook until onions are soft, about 15 to 20 minutes, stirring constantly to prevent onions turning dark. They should be bright pink. Once finished cooking, spread onions in a shallow pan and refrigerate. Pairs great with fried green tomatoes.

Restaurant Recipe

## *Must-Have Patty Melt*

**4 medium yellow onions, sliced**
**2 pounds cremini mushrooms, sliced**
**¼ pound butter plus more for toast**
**2 pounds ground beef, formed into 4 (8-ounce) patties**
**Salt and pepper to taste**
**8 thick slices marble rye bread**
**8 slices Swiss cheese**
**Mayonnaise to taste**

In a large saucepan, combine onion and mushrooms with butter; sauté over medium-low heat, stirring occasionally, until onions are soft and just browning. Remove from heat and cover. Season beef patties with salt and pepper, making sure patties are thin. In a large cast-iron skillet over medium heat, cook patties to medium doneness, about 3 minutes each side. Butter 1 side each slice bread and toast, buttered side down, in a large pan over medium heat until golden brown. Melt 1 slice Swiss over unbuttered sides of toast. To assemble: on bottom toast, squeeze mayonnaise over cheese. Add a scoop mushroom-onion mix. Add patty. Add more mushroom-onion mix. Top with another slice of toasted rye, Swiss side down, and enjoy.

Restaurant Recipe

# Ceviche's

Inspired Panamanian Restaurant & Bar

**7210 Wrightsville Avenue**
**Wilmington, NC 28403**
**910-256-3131**
**www.wbceviche.com • Find us on Facebook**

Inspired by his upbringing in Central America, owner Hunter Tiblier opened Ceviche's to bring a taste of Panama to Wilmington. As a kid, Tiblier fished with his father in the Pacific and Atlantic Oceans, picked fresh mangos at the bus stop for breakfast, and enjoyed epic surfing trips. He wished to bring that feeling to Wrightsville Beach, accompanied by the staples in the Panamanian diet: ceviche, tropical fruit, plantains, and more! Enjoy tapas, like pollo empanadas and coconut shrimp. Don't miss out on the chorizo burger served with yucca fries. You can't forget your drink. Try a house margarita. Visit Ceviche's today for food that is delicious, healthy, and refreshing.

## *Sea Love Margarita*

**Sea Love citrus sea salt**
**Ice to taste**
**1½ ounces top-shelf tequila of choice (e.g., Lunazul Primero)**
**½ ounce freshly squeezed lime juice**
**½ ounce simple syrup**
**½ ounce Grand Marnier liqueur**
**Sliced lime wheels for garnish**

Sprinkle sea salt over a plate; wet rim of margarita glass, dip into salt to coat, add ice and set aside. In a cocktail shaker, add tequila, lime juice and simple syrup; shake to combine and pour into prepared glass. Top with Grand Marnier and garnish rim with a lime wheel.

**Restaurant Recipe**

Lunch:
**Tuesday – Saturday: 11:00 am to 3:00 pm**
Dinner:
**Monday – Saturday: 5:00 pm to 9:30 pm**

## *Ropa Vieja*

**1½ yellow onions, divided**
**1 (2.5-pound) flank steak**
**2 cloves garlic**
**1 tablespoon salt**
**1 tablespoon black pepper corns**
**2 tablespoons oregano, divided**
**2 bay leaves**
**½ cup Worcestershire sauce, divided**
**½ cup red wine, divided**
**¼ cup olive oil**
**1 red onion, julienned**
**1 red bell pepper, julienned**
**1 green bell pepper, julienned**
**½ cup tomato sauce**
**¼ cup red wine vinegar**
**1 cup olives**
**1 cup green peas**
**1 Roma tomato, julienned**

Rough chop ½ yellow onion; add chopped onion to a large stockpot with steak, garlic, salt, pepper corns, 1 tablespoon oregano, bay leaves, ¼ cup Worcestershire and ¼ cup red wine. Add water to cover ingredients by 2 inches, then bring to a boil. Reduce to simmer and cook 3 hours or until flank steak is falling apart. Strain out steak and other ingredients, reserving broth and steak; slice steak into 3-inch sections. Add olive oil to another stockpot. Julienne remaining yellow onion and add to stockpot with red onion, red bell pepper, green bell pepper and remaining oregano; sweat in olive oil over high heat 8 to 10 minutes, stirring frequently. Add steak, remaining red wine, remaining Worcestershire, tomato sauce, red wine vinegar and reserved broth to pot with vegetables; bring to a boil, reduce to simmer and cook 30 minutes. Add olives, peas and Roma tomato; let sit 5 minutes, then serve over coconut rice or white rice.

**Restaurant Recipe**

# The George on the Riverwalk

**128 South Water Street**
**Wilmington, NC 28401**
**910-763-2052**
**www.thegeorgerestaurant.com • Find us on Facebook**

Located in the heart of Downtown Wilmington, on the bank of the historic Cape Fear River, The George on the Riverwalk serves up the best in Southern coastal cuisine, including fresh local seafood, steaks, pasta, salads, and even rotating daily specials. In August 2004, The George opened, serving Caribbean fusion surrounded by art deco decor. In later years, the restaurant found its niche in Southern coastal cuisine, churning out classics like shrimp and grits, bacon-encrusted scallops, and tuna tartare. Even the decor changed, evolving from bright pastels of coral and sea-foam green to sleeker shades of black, gray, and silver. Drop by for riverside dining and impressive bar selections.

**Hours May Vary Seasonally**

## *George's Shrimp & Grits*

**9 extra jumbo shrimp**
**Blackening seasoning to taste**
**2 teaspoons vegetable oil blend, divided**
**2 teaspoons minced shallots**
**1 teaspoon minced garlic**
**½ cup sliced scallions plus more for garnish**
**3 slices bacon, cooked and chopped**
**¼ cup dry white wine**
**½ cup heavy cream**
**Salt and black pepper to taste**
**7 ounces cooked white-cheddar grits**
**½ cup diced tomato for garnish**
**2 tablespoons shredded Parmesan cheese for garnish**

Peel and devein shrimp, removing tails too. Lightly toss in blackening seasoning; sauté in 1 teaspoon vegetable oil in a skillet over medium heat until cooked through. In a shallow pan over medium-high heat, sauté shallots, garlic and ½ cup scallions in remaining oil until soft; fold in bacon, wine and heavy cream, then season to taste with blackening season, salt and pepper. Reduce heat and simmer 4 to 6 minutes or until sauce thickens. Toss shrimp in sauce to fully coat and serve over grits with a garnish of tomatoes, scallions and Parmesan.

**Restaurant Recipe**

## *Southern Chicken Salad*

**2 pounds chicken breasts**
**1 red onion, diced**
**1 cup celery, diced**
**2 cups mayonnaise**
**1 cup sour cream**
**1 tablespoon salt**
**1 teaspoon black pepper**
**1 tablespoon garlic powder**
**1 teaspoon onion powder**

In a large stockpot, boil chicken until cooked through and juices run clear; cool and dice into ¼- to ½-inch cubes. Combine chicken with onion, celery, mayonnaise, sour cream, salt, black pepper, garlic powder and onion powder; stir until evenly blended. Cover and refrigerate at least 4 hours to allow flavors to marinate. Serve over salad or in a croissant bun.

**Family Favorite**

# Kornerstone Bistro

**8262 Market Street**
**Wilmington, NC 28411**
**910-686-2296**
**www.kornerstonebistro.com**
**Find us on Facebook**

Opened in 2007, Kornerstone Bistro is an upscale, casual Italian-Mediterranean bistro that specializes in producing fresh, healthy dishes based on the Mediterranean philosophy of highlighting the flavors of the freshest ingredients. The food is healthy by nature, with a foundation of olive oil, tomato, lemon, whole grains, and coastal North Carolina's bounty. Kornerstone was inspired by the cuisine and culture of the French, Spanish, and Italian Rivieras. Come enjoy a well-prepared meal in a casual atmosphere, relaxing by the bar, on the pet-friendly patio, or by the cozy wood-fired oven. Kornerstone Bistro is your local place for worldly taste.

**Monday – Thursday 11:00 am to 9:00 pm**
**Friday & Saturday 11:00 am – 10:00 pm**
**Sunday 9:30 am – 9:00 pm**

## Mediterranean Flounder

*Lemon Vinaigrette:*

**¼ cup lemon juice**
**1 tablespoon honey**
**1 teaspoon chopped garlic**
**½ cup extra virgin olive oil**
**1 tablespoon chopped parsley**
**Salt and white pepper to taste**

In a bowl, whisk together lemon juice, honey and garlic. While whisking, slowly pour in olive oil. Stir in remaining ingredients.

*Taboulleh:*

**6 cups quinoa**
**4 cups freshly chopped parsley**
**½ cup freshly chopped mint**
**1 cup chickpeas**
**1 cup diced tomato**
**1 cup diced cucumber**
**Salt and pepper to taste**
**4 cups arugula**

Cook quinoa according to package directions; toss in a bowl with next 5 ingredients plus 4 tablespoons Lemon Vinaigrette. Season with salt and pepper and toss with arugula.

*Flounder:*

**4 (6- to 8-ounce) flounder fillets**
**Flour seasoned with salt and pepper**
**¼ cup olive oil**
**½ cup white wine**
**1 tablespoon lemon juice**
**1½ cups diced tomatoes**
**4 tablespoon feta cheese**
**¼ cup sliced Kalamata olives**
**Salt and white pepper to taste**
**1 teaspoon chilled butter**

Dredge fillets in flour; shake off excess. In a large skillet over medium-high heat, add olive oil and fillets; sauté 3 minutes each side until golden brown. Add wine; reduce 2 minutes. Add remaining ingredients except butter. Add butter and gently swirl skillet to incorporate. Adjust seasonings; set aside. Mound Taboullah on plates and lay fillets over top. Divide Flounder sauce between plates, ladling over top of fillets.

**Restaurant Recipe**

# RESTAURANT INDEX

## A



## B



## C

## D

Come In
WE'RE
OPEN

## N



## O



## P

## R



## S

# RECIPE INDEX

## A



## B

## C

## D



## E



## F

## G



## H



## I



## J



## K



## L

## Q

## T

## V



## W

# MORE GREAT AMERICAN BOOKS

**My Notebook Series**

**Alabama • Georgia • Mississippi**

$14.95 • wire-o-bound • 5⅜ x 8¼ • 192 pages

---

*Farm to Table Fabulous* is a back-to-basics approach to cooking and entertaining. This easy-to-follow cookbook will guide you through the seasons with 12 monthly menus for preparing delicious step-by-step meals and tips for hosting a dinner party any month of the year. Using the freshest ingredients for cooking and decorating, you'll create a casual yet enchanting experience for your guests... one they will talk about for years to come.

**Farm to Table Fabulous**
**$18.95 • 256 pages • 7x9**
**paperbound • full color**

## Church Recipes are the Best

**Georgia Church Suppers**
$18.95 • 256 pages • 7x10 • paperbound • full color

**Mississippi Church Suppers**
$21.95 • 288 pages • 7x10 • paperbound • full color

---

**Little Gulf Coast Seafood Cookbook**
$14.95 • 192 pages • 5½x8½
paperbound • full color

---

**The Ultimate Venison Cookbook for Deer Camp**
$21.95 • 288 pages • 7x10
paperbound • full color

---

**Game for all Seasons Cookbook**
$16.95 • 240 pages • 7x10
paperbound • full color

**Kids in the Kitchen**
$18.95 • 256 pages
x10 • paperbound • full color

**Great American Grilling**
$21.95 • 288 pages • 7x10
paperbound • full color

**Betty B's Having a Party!**
**A Holiday Dinner Party Cookbook**
$18.95 • 256 pages • 7x9
paperbound • full color

---

## State Hometown Cookbook Series

***A Hometown Taste of America, One State at a Time***

EACH: $18.95 • 240 to 272 pages • 7x10 • paperbound

Alabama • Georgia • Louisiana • Mississippi
South Carolina • Tennessee • Texas • West Virginia

---

## Eat & Explore Cookbook Series

***Discover community celebrations and unique destinations, as they share their favorite recipes.***

EACH: $18.95 • 256 pages • 7x9 • paperbound

Arkansas • Illinois • Minnesota • North Carolina
Ohio • Oklahoma • Virginia • Washington

**www.GreatAmericanPublishers.com • www.facebook.com/GreatAmericanPublishers**

# State Back Road Restaurant Recipes Cookbook Series

From two-lane highways and interstates, to dirt roads and qu downtowns, every road leads to delicious food when traveling ac our United States. The STATE BACK ROAD RESTAURANT REC COOKBOOK SERIES serves up a well-researched and charming g to each state's best back road restaurants. No time to travel? No p lem. Each restaurant shares with you their favorite recipes—s times their signature dish, sometimes a family favorite, but a delicious.

**EACH: $18.95 • 256 pages • 7x9 • paperbound • full-col**

**Arkansas • Kentucky • Louisiana • Missouri • North Carolin**
**Oklahoma • South Carolina • Tennessee • Texas**

## 3 Easy Ways to Order

1) Call toll-free **1-888-854-5954** to order by phone or to request a free catalog.

2) Order online at **www.GreatAmericanPublishers.com**

3) Mail a check or money order for the cost of the book(s) plus $5 shipping for the first book and $1 each additional plus a list of the books you want to order along with your name, address, phone and email to:

Great American Publishers
171 Lone Pine Church Road
Lena MS 39094

Find us on facebook: www.facebook.com/GreatAmericanPublishers

**Join the We Love 2 Cook Club and get a 10% discount.**
**www.GreatAmericanPublishers.com**